$ 7.70

HAYEK

Hayek

HIS CONTRIBUTION TO
THE POLITICAL AND ECONOMIC
THOUGHT OF OUR TIME

*

EAMONN BUTLER

UNIVERSE BOOKS
NEW YORK

Published in the United States of America in 1985
by Universe Books
381 Park Avenue South, New York, N.Y. 10016

85 86 87 88 89 / 10 9 8 7 6 5 4 3 2 1

Printed in the United States of America

Library of Congress Cataloging in Publication Data

Butler, Eamonn.
    Hayek, his contribution to the political and economic
thought of our time.

    Bibliography: p.
    Includes index.
    1. Hayek, Friedrich A. von (Friedrich August),
1899–   2.Economics — History — 20th century.
I. Title.
HB101.H39B87   1985   330.1   84-28037
ISBN 0-87663-475-7
ISBN 0-87663-877-9 (pbk.)

Contents

Preface

AT a recent meeting of the Carl Menger Society (a group devoted to the understanding of the 'Austrian School' of economics), the works of F.A. Hayek were being discussed. As usual, the Alternative Bookshop had brought along a wide selection of the works of Hayek and other members of the school. But as the many people present who had no background in economics or political science looked over the books, some were intimidated by the technical content of several of them, and the remainder had to ask where the general reader should start. This incident made it clear to me that there was an urgent need for an introduction to Hayek's thought which covered his main arguments but which could be understood by the general reader or the student who did not have a social sciences background.

To summarise the often complex arguments of over 25 books in one volume must inevitably require some oversimplification, and no doubt my friends in the academic community will argue that I have distorted Hayek's arguments in the process. But it is to me the discharge of an intellectual duty to present the essentials of Hayek's thought without any resort to intimidating technical language, so enabling a much wider audience to understand his work instead of knowing only his name.

I would like to thank my friends at the Adam Smith Institute for their help and advice on the manuscript: Dr Madsen Pirie and Mr Russell Walters.

The Adam Smith Institute, London

INTRODUCTION

Hayek's Life and Work

> . . . we must shed the illusion that we can deliberately
> 'create the future of mankind'. . . This is the final
> conclusion of the forty years which I have now devoted
> to the study of these problems. . .[1]

FRIEDRICH HAYEK's influence in helping a generation to understand the nature of a liberal[2] society and the errors of collectivism goes far beyond that of any writer of his period.

Before and after the second world war, the intellectual tide swept unceasingly in the direction of socialism. The consensus of the age was for economic planning, the setting of targets for economic growth, full employment policy, comprehensive state welfare services, and the redistribution of incomes. It was a consensus which Hayek never joined.[3] Indeed, it was he who showed in *The Road to Serfdom* that even the most modest dalliance with these ideas would lead to disaster if they were pursued consistently. His clear book, and the condensed version of it which reached millions,[4] achieved a major and demonstrable change in the minds of many men of thought and of action.

When the worst implications of the political consensus were becoming plain, Hayek gave powerful ammunition to the supporters of the free society in his statement of its principles, *The Constitution of Liberty*; and later in *Law, Legislation and Liberty* he set out the legal and constitutional framework needed to support the delicate structure of the liberal social order.

His contribution, therefore, is in line with his belief that all of the great social movements have been led not by politicians but by men of ideas. And yet his practical influence is increased by the fact that many prominent people in the world of politics have not only read his works, but have been moved by them.

1

HAYEK'S LIFE

Hayek's family had a strong tradition of scholarship in the natural sciences. One grandfather was a zoologist, the other (after a time as professor of constitutional law) was a statistician and president of the Statistical Commission of Austria. His father, a doctor of medicine, turned to research and teaching as professor of botany at the University of Vienna. One brother became professor of anatomy at Vienna, the other, professor of chemistry at Innsbruck. So although economic issues fascinated him, as a young man Hayek was uncertain whether to become an economist or a psychologist. But despite his eventual movement away from the sciences, the family tradition continued: his daughter became a biologist and his son a bacteriologist.

Born in Vienna on 8 May 1899, Hayek undoubtedly benefited from his intellectual environment. He knew the great economist, Eugen von Böhm-Bawerk, for example, as a friend of his grandfather even before he had learnt the meaning of the word 'economics'. It was scarcely surprising that he should enter the University of Vienna, and hardly less so that he should receive two doctorates, in law (1921) and in political science (1923).

He was just old enough to glimpse the imperial civilisation of Austria which was extinguished by the first world war, and even to serve in the armed forces (although he later claimed that his only lasting memory of the conflict was that of trying to recapture a bucketful of eels which were meant for the breakfast of the troops, but which he had accidentally overturned in a dewy field). But the turmoil of the wartime period diverted him away from the natural sciences, and made him take up the economic and social issues on which his reputation would come to be based.

As a research student he had visited the United States, although the free enterprise economy of that country does not seem to have made much of an impact on the moderate, Fabian socialist views he held at the time. He has speculated that this mild socialism proved of value to him in the long term, because he had to work out the principles of a free society for himself,

2

deliberating over every point. In this, he was helped by the leading economist of the 'Austrian' school, Ludwig von Mises.[5]

As one of the directors of a temporary government office, Mises was looking for young lawyers and economists. At his interview, Mises remarked that he had never seen Hayek at his lectures on economics (almost true: Hayek had looked in once but found Mises's lecture conspicuously antipathetic to his mild socialist ideas) but hired him nonetheless. For the next five years, Mises was Hayek's chief in the office, and after that he became vice-president of the Austrian Institute for Economic Research, an institute to study business cycles and economic policy which they started together and of which Hayek became director. In addition to this work, Hayek spent the years between 1929 and 1931 lecturing in economics at the University of Vienna.

This was undoubtedly a period of important intellectual development as Mises weaned Hayek off his Fabian views. In the *Privateseminar* discussion group which met in Mises's office, he began to understand the problems of socialism, and was completely won over by Mises's stinging critique, *Socialism*, which appeared in German in 1922.[6]

It was also a time when Hayek was coming into contact with many of the great economists of the age. In London in 1928, for example, he first met John Maynard Keynes, with whom he conducted a public and private debate on the importance of money for the next twenty years. It was a subject which Hayek had definite views about: he had, after all, been in a job where his salary was increased 200 times in eight months to keep up with prices which doubled each day.[7] And he became an acknowledged expert on the subject with the German publication of *Monetary Theory and the Trade Cycle* in 1929.

London: Lionel (later Lord) Robbins was also impressed with Hayek, and arranged for him to give a series of lectures at the London School of Economics in 1931, soon afterwards published as *Prices and Production*. Later that year, Hayek was appointed Tooke Professor of Economic Science and Statistics at the University of London, where he remained until 1950. The values which he found in Britain impressed him so much that he became a naturalised British subject in 1938, just a few weeks before German forces invaded his native Austria.

In 1931 and 1932 he devoted much energy and time to a critical review of Keynes's *Treatise on Money*, only to be told by its author that he had changed his mind completely on the subject in the meantime. Largely because he suspected that Keynes would change his mind yet again, Hayek did not attempt a systematic refutation of Keynes's next and most influential work, the *General Theory*.[8] It was a mistake for which Hayek much blamed himself in later years.

His friendship with Keynes, however, continued throughout the war years. In 1940, when the London School of Economics was moved for safety to Cambridge, Keynes found quarters for Hayek at his college, and thus they came to know each other even better on a personal as well as professional level.

Hayek's studies of pure economic theory continued with such works as *The Pure Theory of Capital* in 1941, but social and political questions were occupying his mind more and more. It was, he says, as a result of his impotence to stop German bombs falling over London that he wrote 'Scientism and the Study of Society' and the other essays comprising *The Counter-Revolution of Science*, a stinging attack on the overvaunting use of 'scientific' methods in social studies. Because he feared that unworkable socialist utopian ideas based on this misunderstanding of society were gaining strength in Britain at this time, he published *The Road to Serfdom* in 1944. To his surprise, it was an instant and major success both in Britain and the United States. Hayek the respected economist had suddenly been transformed into Hayek the controversial social theorist.

But the timing was perhaps fortunate. Just a few months before the publication of the book, which shattered the then prevalent complacent belief in moderate socialism, Hayek was elected as a fellow of the British Academy. His friend Sir John Clapham told Hayek that if the publication had been in July rather than September, he would never have been elected a member, such was the intellectual tenor of the times.

The Mont Pelerin Society: It was at a meeting chaired by Sir John Clapham in King's College, Cambridge, in 1944 that Hayek floated an idea which was to have a lasting significance. The problem was how to rebuild the intellectual foundations of the free society that had been forgotten during the war and, particularly, how to harness the energies of academics from all the warring nations to the task.

Hayek's solution was an international society; and due principally to his energies, 39 academics and others came together in 1947 at Mont Pelerin in Switzerland to discuss the principles of the liberal order and how they might be preserved.[9]

Since that time, the Mont Pelerin Society (as it came to be called) has held international or regional meetings almost every year, and in more than a dozen countries. At its meeting in Berlin in 1982, Hayek noted that he had missed only two meetings, one through ill health and another (characteristically) when he felt that his presence might prejudice the discussions going on. The Society had met in Berlin once before, in 1954, when many of the great liberal minds of the time – Hayek, Ludwig Erhard, Mises, Alfred Müller-Armack and others – had taken a bus trip into the Eastern sector. Having made it safely back once, Hayek did not attempt the trip again in 1982!

The discussions of the Mont Pelerin Society have always had an influence far beyond those who have taken part as members or guests. Arising out of papers read to the 1951 meeting in France, for example, came the volume *Capitalism and the Historians*, which Hayek edited, and which painstakingly refuted the widespread myth that early capitalism brought only poverty and misery to the downtrodden workers. Many other papers from Mont Pelerin Society meetings over the years have been published in books and scholarly journals. Yet it would not be an exaggeration to say that the most important function of the society is to continue the debate and development of the ideas of liberty, and to provide a meeting place for those, young and old and of many different nationalities and backgrounds, who wish to be part of that development.

Hayek at Chicago: In 1950, partly because of divorce and the strain of maintaining two households, but principally because of the new horizons which it offered, Hayek took up an appointment at the University of Chicago. He had been surprised at the success of *The Road to Serfdom* in America, where it sold at an unprecedented rate for such a work, particularly since it had been written for a European readership.[10] Significantly, the American publication had been undertaken by the University of Chicago, where at that time the famous 'Chicago School' of economics was flourishing. Yet, as if to emphasise that Hayek's ideas were iconclastic even in such a place, or perhaps demonstrating his breadth of thought, he did not join the University as an economics professor, but as professor of social and moral sciences and member of the Committee on Social Thought.

At Chicago, Hayek was (by general agreement) well able to supply the range of interest demanded by such a post, and his emphasis on stimulating the open discussion of the principles of liberty continued. At weekly seminars arranged by him, for example, some of the best minds of the University were able to meet, without barriers of age, status or academic discipline, to discuss topics he proposed.[11]

The breadth of these discussions is paralleled by the wide range of subjects treated in Hayek's next book. *The Constitution of Liberty*, published by the University of Chicago in 1960. It is a major, systematic statement of the arguments for and the principles of individual liberty. Its mixture of academic analysis and practical recommendations on health, education, welfare, planning and other policies guaranteed it the widest audience and an influence which continues to this day.

Germany and Austria: Having spent 31 of his most productive years in the English-speaking world, Hayek accepted an appointment as Professor of Economic Policy at the University of Freiburg in 1962. The University that had been the intellectual home of Walter Eucken and his neo-liberal colleagues was undoubtedly a congenial place to him. When he retired in 1967, he accepted an honorary professorship at the University of Salzburg in his home country of Austria, and was awarded other honours for his lifetime's work in philosophy, political science and economics, honours coming from all

aggregates which economists like to talk about. It shows the very complex nature of capital and its importance in economic booms and slumps, and stands as a classic in the field. Sadly, Hayek's theories were soon overshadowed by the prominence which Keynes achieved in the intellectual and political world, providing politicians with apparently softer options than Hayek would have prescribed. But inevitably, after many decades, reality had to break through.

Economic policy fascinated Hayek as much as its pure theory, as evidenced by his contribution as editor to *Collectivist Economic Planning* (1935). This took up Mises's forceful discovery that the problem of knowing how best to use resources, faced by every socialist planner, was insuperable. It was a point which Hayek was to develop so effectively in *The Road to Serfdom* nine years later.

Hayek went on to discuss this problem of calculation in the collectivist economy. *Individualism and Economic Order* (1948) contains a number of his essays on the problems of socialist calculation, exploring the various ways (including the use of prices and competition) which socialist states have or can employ to solve the difficulties of allocating resources efficiently. The same book contains other essays on the nature of the individualist philosophy and the strategy of the social sciences.

This theme was taken up again in *The Counter-Revolution of Science* (1952). It explains with remarkable accuracy and detail the problems and the mistakes which arise when we attempt to use the methods of the physical sciences in social study. For not only is society a complex phenomenon, says Hayek, and therefore quite unlike the simple models studied in the physical sciences, but each individual making up that complex structure is himself complex and impossible to predict with any accuracy. The problem for any planner is that the 'facts' he must deal with are not concrete things, but are the relationships and behaviour of individuals themselves, something which nobody can predict in advance. It is a poor basis for any social 'science': while we might be able to talk about some general patterns of society, we should never suppose that we can completely predict it.

The Road to Serfdom (1944) is, on the author's own admission, a political book. But it is nevertheless a work of considerable scholarship, in which the implications of the socialist conception are painstakingly spelt out. It argues that many 'democratic' socialists have a utopian ideal that would be glorious if it could be achieved. But even a modest amount of economic planning requires coercive machinery to force people to act in certain ways, according to the plans that are decided on. Hayek says that this is a recipe for arbitrary government: instead of treating people equally, the socialist planner has to treat them as mere instruments for the achievement of the economic plan. Fairly soon, the grip of the planning agency over the lives and ambitions of individuals must become more and more complete, and the power embodied in it attracts political leaders with fewer scruples than the socialist idealists. Thus, moderate socialists find themselves drawn down a road which none of them want, and only the abandonment of their ideals will avoid the drift to totalitarianism.

The Constitution of Liberty (1960) is a massive restatement of the principles and practice of liberalism in modern terms. It shows how society is a complex thing, beyond the capability of any single mind to understand and therefore impossible to plan. Individual freedom is needed if it is to develop and be sustained, and any attempt to inhibit freedom will rob the social order of its unique ability to allocate resources efficiently and to overcome new challenges and problems. The book examines the legal framework which is required to support this liberal society, introducing Hayek's idea of the rule of law: treating people equally instead of as pieces in an economic chess game. And it examines some of the economic institutions which are necessary to build a humane society with the minimum of coercion. As such, many readers with a background in practical affairs rather than in political philosophy have found it to be a useful introduction to Hayek's thought, and it is not therefore surprising that its influence has been so widespread.

Law, Legislation and Liberty, in three volumes (1973, 1976 and 1979), develops the earlier work to explore the legal arrangements which are necessary in the free society. It shows how the roots of social life can be found in human evolution (rather than in conscious planning), exposes the lack of precision of 'social' or redistributive justice, and puts forward suggestions for a constitutional arrangement which would keep down the arbitrary powers of government authority. Despite the fact that the three volumes display a certain lack of system, having been composed over fifteen years or so and having been interrupted by a period of ill health, *Law, Legislation and Liberty* develops some fascinating themes briefly outlined in *The Constitution of Liberty*, making it the subject of much fruitful academic debate.

These two works demonstrate the increasing importance in Hayek's thought of the unplanned nature of society. The institutions of the economy and of social life are indeed the results of human action, he argues, but are not the products of human design and planning. On the contrary, the institutions which shape society arise quite spontaneously when men meet and trade together. The law, such as the law of contract, which allows people to do this is essentially *discovered*, not made by wise men: we discover what will work, and abandon what does not. The socialist assumption that we can scrap these laws, which are general ones applying to everyone, and move to a command economy is, in the title of Hayek's attack on it, *The Fatal Conceit*. Property, contract, honesty and other values are ingrained in us because they work; they allow a free society to operate. It is a conceit to suppose that we can replace these universal values with a council of wise men who will tell us how to act in every situation and who will direct us individually for the achievement of some social or economic plan. The socialist ideals of sharing and effort towards common goals may appeal to our instincts, since they were obviously important in our hunting and tribal past. But they cannot work in the large societies of today, which have grown far beyond the scope of any one mind to control.

HAYEK'S CHARACTER AND INFLUENCE

Through his writings and teaching, Hayek has had a very great influence on intellectual debate in economics and political science. Yet he has always avoided being part of anything like a 'school' or a 'movement'. Although he inspired the Mont Pelerin Society and was its president until 1960 (and honorary president thereafter), he occasionally contemplated winding it up – in case it became too much of a proselytising body – according to his friend and follower Arthur Shenfield.[14]

To some extent, this reticence disappeared after he won the Nobel Prize, when his views and opinions were in demand all over the world. But his doubt about the practice of politics, and his belief that it is ideas and not politicians which really shape society in the long run, never wavered.

He provided his own illustration of this view. When a young Battle of Britain pilot, Antony Fisher, read *The Road to Serfdom*, he was moved by it sufficiently to ask Hayek whether he should go into politics to resist the evils Hayek had anticipated. Hayek advised him to avoid politics, and do what he could in the field of ideas. Some years later, in 1956, Fisher (now a successful businessman) founded the Institute of Economic Affairs, a body which succeeded in overturning the economic consensus in Britain, and which helped change the minds of a generation of students in economics. Its success is now being emulated in similar institutes throughout the world.

No person who has met Hayek could deny that his principal interest is ideas, and not the cut and thrust of politics and much academic life. He takes an obvious delight in hearing a new point of view, and of quickly and delightedly exploring its implications along many lines of thought with an agility and economy which is the envy of many younger men. Although he suffers deafness in his left ear (he points out that Karl Marx was deaf in his right), he remains a keen contributor to discussion and debate, possessing the rare gift of being able to cut cleanly and swiftly through tangled arguments to the very heart of the subject.

Hayek's manners both in print and in person are impeccable. Indeed, the economist J.A. Schumpeter once accused him of politeness to a fault, because he hardly ever attributed to opponents anything beyond intellectual error.[15] While at Chicago, it was noted that he was never one to build his own empire, diverting resources and encouragement to his research students, and treating the results of his researches as if they were common property.

Indeed, Hayek has written that knowledge is something that it is hard to claim ownership over, since others can absorb it free of charge; so this attitude is very much in line with his written thoughts. He has also written that it is the little qualities of personality which are so important in fostering good relations between men and therefore crucial in making the liberal society possible; values such as kindliness and a sense of humour, personal modesty and respect for other people's good intentions.[16] One might add punctuality and reliability, and then Hayek could be the model himself: for those who know him are agreed that in his writings and in person he approaches as near to the ideal of the liberal scholar as perhaps human frailty will admit.

CHAPTER ONE

Understanding how Society Works

If we are to understand how society works, we must
attempt to define the general nature and range of our
ignorance concerning it.[1]

THROUGHOUT his writings, Hayek points to a very common but
mistaken belief about the way in which social institutions work.
Put simply, this is the belief that since man has himself created
the institutions of society and civilisation (such as the law,
moral codes and social institutions), he must also be able to
alter them at will so as to satisfy his desires or wishes.[2]

At first, this view seems very reasonable and rather
encouraging. It suggests that if we want to build a better
society, we are quite able to scrap our existing laws, values and
institutions and replace them with ones which will bring about
a more desirable state of affairs. After all, we created our
institutions, so we can change them. But Hayek maintains that
this view rests on a deep misunderstanding of the true origins of
social life and institutions, and that the reconstruction of
society which it supposes to be possible would therefore be the
gravest error. It would be like building on quicksand.

ORDER WITHOUT COMMANDS

The view that our institutions are infinitely malleable rests on
the misleading division of things into those which are 'natural'
and those which are 'artificial'. It is a distinction which has
been made since the ancient Greeks,[3] but in Hayek's view it is a
false distinction, which arises from our inaccurate use of
language in everyday life. For there certainly exists a third
group of things, which are neither exactly 'natural' nor
'artificial', and it is into this group that social institutions
should be placed.

When we speak of something as 'natural', we often give it connotations of being unplanned, irregular, unstructured and wild. The opposite, 'artificial' or 'invented', suggests something that is built for a purpose, structured, regular and planned. Since laws, governments, moral rules and other social institutions are obviously regular in their operation and have an orderly structure, and since they are plainly the results of human action, people tend to suppose that they fall exclusively into the second group: that they are 'invented' and can therefore be re-invented.

Nothing could be further from the truth, insists Hayek. We need a third category to describe social institutions, because although they have a structured appearance, they have *not* been invented or planned. The structures of social life have grown and evolved that way, as the physical structure of a crystal grows or a tree evolves. We did not consciously choose them because we recognised the benefits which they would bring; but they have evolved and survived because they do bring benefits to those groups of people who adopt them. While these structures are undoubtedly patterns of human behavior, they are not the consequence of human design or planning.[4]

This is a difficult notion to grasp, so long have we been misled by the common use of the words 'natural' and 'artificial'; but it is important if we are to realise how little we understand about the workings of society, and how much our understanding is itself the *product* of civilisation, not its inventor or master. Wild men did not just come together to reason out and invent a set of social rules. On the contrary, it was the benefits of living in groups which made men evolve as rational, rule-guided creatures. When people argue that we should use our minds to restructure social institutions, they fail to see that the structure of those minds and of society have evolved together.[5]

Examples of unplanned orders: Hayek cites a number of examples of phenomena which are orderly but not the result of planning. Human language is one: it has a complex grammatical structure, words are used in a consistent fashion, and different speakers are in general agreement about the meaning of words and phrases. Yet nobody would argue that language was 'invented' by a rational being, despite its regularities and despite the obvious benefits it confers on those who use it. It has simply *grown* and survived because it is useful.

Animal societies provide plenty of examples of orderly conduct.[6] The complex societies of bees or termites, with their division of labour between the various individuals, make up an impressive overall order. But we would not wish to say that any particular bee or termite knew how its behaviour contributed to the overall pattern, nor that this overall pattern was in any way 'planned'.

The wearing away of a footpath across a field is another example of how individual action can produce a beneficial but unplanned outcome. The purpose of walking in someone else's tracks is to make the walk easier; it is purely selfish. But after a few people have done this, they have worn away a hard path which eases the journey of everyone in the future. The creation of the footpath was nobody's intention, but the fortunate result of their private ambitions to take the easiest route.[7]

INDIVIDUAL BEHAVIOUR AND SOCIAL ORDER

These examples do not show us only that complex structures can come to exist without being consciously designed. They illustrate a point which is crucial to understanding Hayek's view of society: that there is a major and distinct difference between the regularities of individual conduct and the overall regularities of society which they produce. The worker bee, for example, performs different activities such as foraging, cell-cleaning and so on at different stages in its life; and so we can say that its behaviour is regular or can be described by rules. Although the bee may not even realise that its actions are regular, its behaviour and the behaviour of its fellows contribute to make up a complex insect community. But it is difficult to estimate how a change in the behaviour of the individuals (such as spending more time on foraging, less on cell-cleaning) would affect the overall shape of the community, because they are two different things and are related in a rather complex way.

Or to take the example of the footpath again, although the

17

motives of the individuals were purely selfish, they nevertheless serve to produce a situation which *appears* to be a co-operative one. The relationship between individual behaviour and the social pattern it produces is therefore by no means a straightforward one.

It is for this reason that Hayek warns us against the belief that we can reconstruct social institutions at will. Our understanding of how the regularities of individual conduct and the rules of morality, of law and of habit, are related to the regularity of the social order is a weak one at best. By asking people to change their behaviour, we might unwittingly destroy the complex overall order which we were hoping to improve:

... before we can try to remould society intelligently, we must understand its functioning; we must realize that, even when we believe that we understand it, we may be mistaken. What we must learn to understand is that human civilization has a life of its own, that all our efforts to improve things must operate within a working whole which we cannot entirely control, and the operation of whose forces we can hope merely to facilitate and assist so far as we can understand them.[8]

Rules and order: The task of social and political studies, then, is to discover what sorts of action at the individual level will in fact bring about a smoothly functioning social order. For an unplanned order or pattern to exist, says Hayek, there has to be some degree of regularity in the behaviour of the individuals themselves, since random behaviour of the individuals would not produce a stable order. Hayek calls these regularities *rules*, not implying that the individuals are following any commands laid down, nor even that they realise they act in a certain way: but just to indicate that their behaviour follows certain discoverable principles.

But for an overall social pattern to emerge and survive through evolution does not necessarily require that the individuals themselves should all act in precisely the same way or have a common purpose. Even a very limited similarity of action may be sufficient: for example, rules *against* injuring others, or theft of property, or breaking promises, may well make co-operation and social life possible but leave each individual a great deal of scope for free action. And, of course, most social rules, moral codes, customs and laws work in precisely this way, *prohibiting* certain actions but leaving the vast bulk of possible behaviour untouched.[9] And as for the point about common purpose, the footpath example shows that it need not exist for a beneficial effect to arise. We do not have to suppose that there is some miraculous natural harmony of personal interests in order to explain how smooth social orders arise.[10] Quite selfish behaviour can sometimes produce this result.

But the person who thinks that we can reconstruct society according to our wishes must note that not every regularity of individual behaviour will produce an overall order. As Hayek says, a rule that an individual should try to kill any other he encountered, or flee as soon as he saw another, would clearly make any social order impossible. Although this may be an extreme example, there will obviously be many other more plausible rules which might appear on the surface to be conducive to a functioning society, but which would in practice lead to its breakdown. The snag is that the relationship between the individual rules and the resulting overall order is so complex and unfathomable that we cannot tell in advance which sets of rules will work and which will not.

The only guide we have is what has worked in the past. The systems of rules of individual conduct that produce an order will bring the benefits of co-operation to people and allow the groups following those rule systems to expand. Deliberately changing any one of those rules may upset the delicate interrelationship between them and lead to chaos; we can never be quite sure. Hayek is not an inflexible conservative and does not argue that we should leave our moral and legal rules exactly the way they are: on the contrary, as circumstances change, he says, our practices have to evolve and adapt to them. But he does point out that our existing, inherited institutions serve their own functions in making society possible, in ways which we can often hardly guess at. They contain, as it were, a certain wisdom, *a knowledge of how to act.* Those who wish to abandon all existing rules and substitute others are mistaken because they do not realise this; but the knowledge content of the rules forms the foundation of the next major stage in Hayek's explanation of the structure of society.

THE KNOWLEDGE CONTENT OF RULES

Hayek takes a very wide view of the meaning of the word 'knowledge'. It is not restricted, he says, merely to 'facts' that are known; the knowledge of 'how to' do things is equally important. Our skills, for example, are important knowledge which we have, but they are knowledge of a sort that cannot be written down in books. Our habits, and even our emotional attitudes and gestures, undoubtedly play an important part in making social life possible, but we do not have to understand them or explain their relevance to society as a whole. We simply follow them, and the knowledge that they contain helps us live and co-operate together without having to think about it. Or again, the tools we use are essential if we are to master our environment, but we are generally ignorant of why our implements are shaped in one way rather than another, for they are the results of the experience of successive generations which are handed down. Every time we discover an improvement, we incorporate it and hand it down to the next generation, and so the implements which they inherit contain our experience and the 'knowledge' of generations before us. And social institutions, traditions, customs, values and other kinds of regular behaviour are just like tools, containing this knowledge of how to act.[11]

Social institutions can thus encapsulate vital information, without this knowledge content ever being understood by the individuals who act within them. We do not have to 'know' why we behave in certain ways or follow particular traditions and customs in order for those rules to be instrumental in producing a social order. They are not so much the result of our deliberate choice in an effort to achieve specific purposes, but of a process of evolutionary selection in which the groups which achieved a more efficient order displaced others, often without knowing to what their superiority was due. Groups in which the various rules adopted fit together like a clockwork to produce an efficient overall order will expand and displace others, without the individuals having to understand the complexity of the mechanism.

The transmission of rules: Behavioural rules are selected at the group level by whether or not they produce a functioning social order; but they are transmitted genetically – emotional dispositions, certain basic facial expressions, and so on. Others have a cultural origin, and Hayek distinguishes three important categories of these.

The first group is those rules which are deliberately chosen. The people who believe that society can be consciously manipulated at will (the *constructivists* as Hayek calls them) argue that these are the most important rules. Since they have been deliberately drawn up, they exist in words and sentences, and can be readily communicated and discussed.

The second group is the rules which we follow, but which we cannot express in words. For example, there are accepted customs of 'fair play' which it would be hard to write down in a rule book, although we can tell when they have been broken. Or again, we can tell if someone has a 'feeling for the language' and follows not only the rules of grammar but achieves good style, even though we cannot put into words what it is which makes good grammar and good style. And even more importantly, we have a 'sense of justice' which tells us when someone is acting according to just principles, even though we cannot explain precisely what those principles are.

This second group of rules, which Hayek clearly thinks is the most important one for social theorists to recognise, comprises rules which can be very complex indeed. It is doubtful, for instance, that anyone could succeed in setting down in words all the things which were covered by the principle of 'fair play'. But in order to be learnt, they do not need to be written down or explained. We see them operating in everyday life, and we can watch how our parents, teachers and colleagues behave in a large number of particular circumstances. From these numerous examples of how to act in thousands of specific circumstances, our minds develop the rules which guide us, linking those cases together into patterns of behaviour and ways of seeing the world which can be of astonishing

21

complexity.[12] Indeed, they are often so complex that the same minds which follow them cannot explain them in words.

The third group of rules are those which are initially learnt by the same process of being observed in action, but which we also try to express in words. The common law, for example, is built up over the centuries and is really a collection of individual judgements and cases which can be used as precedents in future disputes; but we obviously find it useful if we can put into words the principles which link those various judgements together. We can write down a number of such legal principles derived from cases. But our written words are just an attempt to state approximately what has long been generally observed in action, and most judicial decisions, says Hayek, are in fact efforts to articulate rules of justice which are followed in practice but have not been previously written down.[13]

Thus the rules and values which have come down to us have come down through various routes, and we should not therefore make the blind assumption that only articulated, purposefully chosen rules are important.[14] To explain exactly how any biologically evolved structure has come to be the way it is must be a difficult or impossible task. In order to explain why species of organisms have the body structures they do, for example, we would have to know all about the genetic history of the species concerned, and all about the many particular events since the earth's formation which were important in their evolutionary formation. To explain the structure of society is an even more impossible task. We cannot just 'add up' individual behaviour patterns to show how they fit into an overall social order. The overall order of society emerges as a result of the adjustment of the actions of millions of individuals to those of others, with many complex rules of behaviour meshing into one another, and into the rapidly fluctuating current circumstances and past history of the environment.

ADVANTAGES OF RULE-GUIDED SOCIETIES

In a small group of individuals who know each other, it is easy for any one of them to predict how his fellows will variously respond to his actions, and therefore to assess what the overall effect on the group will be. The relationship between the individual's actions and the overall result is straightforward. But in the large, extended society of today, things are very different: the individual will know only a handful of the thousands or millions who comprise the community. To assess the effects of one's actions would be impossible unless most people could be counted on to follow general rules of action, to behave in certain regular and predictable ways. Modern social life therefore depends upon our behaviour being rule-guided. The rules have what Hayek calls an *abstract* nature: they are not followed to achieve a particular result, but are a framework which make social life – and its benefits – available to us.

It would be impossible if we had to stop and calculate the wider implications of all our actions, constantly trying to work out how others would react and how this would affect yet others. Fortunately, rule-guided behaviour does the work for us. Like the acquisition of a skill, which enables us to do something without having to think about it, social institutions such as laws, customs and morals enable us to co-operate with others without having to worry about how to behave. Like skills, they give us an instant and unconscious summary of how to act.[15]

The large society of rule-guided individuals has other advantages in terms of the knowledge, skill and information it can draw upon. Any society which is organised and directed by a central authority, be it a commander, a council of wise men, or even a computer system, is obviously limited by the amount of knowledge which the authority possesses. Whether or not it could react to and survive new environmental changes would depend on whether it had sufficient knowledge in its central mind. Equally important, its structure would be *limited in complexity* to the moderate degree of complication which the central authority could devise and control.[16] Since no mind could explain and control anything more complex than itself,[17] there is bound to be a definite upper limit on the complexity of a centrally directed society; but far below that will be the practical limit of how much knowledge can be handled centrally. While the size and complexity of a centralised society is limited, therefore, very complex social orders, drawing upon more facts than any brain could ascertain or manipulate, are *only* possible where they result from the evolution of systems of rules and *not* from deliberate design.

Where the knowledge of how to act is held by many millions of individuals rather than by some central authority, says Hayek, more information can be made to work. Because individuals can use their own knowledge of local events, they can adjust rapidly to them without having to be directed, and their adjustment is not limited to the knowledge held by some central agency. So the society which is formed by the adoption of general rules of conduct is likely to be far more effective at adjusting to changing circumstances than one which is consciously designed and directed.

Hayek therefore comes to the conclusion that, while it is certainly possible to construct social organisations which are run according to rules of our own choosing, these must necessarily be limited in scope and size. To suppose that we can simply scrap our existing laws and social institutions and substitute new ones of our own choosing certainly risks the demolition of our very complex society to which millions of individuals owe their existence.[18] While we *can* change *some* institutions, it is an exercise which needs the greatest of care.

THE IMPORTANCE OF INDIVIDUAL LIBERTY

Armed with these principles of how complex societies evolve, we can now understand the keystone position occupied by individual freedom or liberty in Hayek's social and political thought.[19] By this, Hayek means the state in which a man is not subject to coercion by the arbitrary will of another; the liberal or free society to which Hayek aims is a society in which the subjugation of individuals to the will of others and the use of coercion are minimised.

Many writers, of course, have argued that freedom is a value in itself, and obviously worth having for its own sake. Hayek would not oppose this view. But he does argue with those who believe that the benefits of freedom can be traded against other things which we also value and which can only be achieved by

24

giving up a measure of liberty. On the contrary, he argues, the deeper and more long-term benefits of social life, to be possible at all, *require* liberty, and he produces a number of arguments to justify such a liberal attitude.[20]

Ignorance: A principal justification of liberty rests on the inevitable ignorance of all of us concerning the many and various factors upon which the achievement of our ends and welfare depend. We simply *do not know* exactly how our actions and institutions contribute to the overall order of society, nor what a change in them would mean. To force people to act in a certain way could therefore disrupt the complex mechanism which brings us many benefits. Although the removal of personal liberty and the ordering of society according to a central plan might promise some benefits, they are more likely to prove disastrous.

Progress and the use of knowledge: Liberty is essential to make room for the unforseeable and unpredictable. Accidents, sometimes lucky accidents, do happen, and often we stumble across new ways of doing things which are better than the old. It is in this way that we learn and make the best use of knowledge available to us. Yet progress cannot be planned for; the most we can do is create the conditions which make it more likely that new discoveries can be made. The person who believes that everything should be planned aims at predictability and control of events, which are quite opposed to any progress being made.[21]

We have to recognise the creative powers which only a free civilisation has. Because they are free to act within the rules which make social life possible, individuals are free to explore and experiment with new ways of doing things. New ideas can be developed, new tools can be fashioned, and changes in particular features of the environment can be adjusted to. The wealth of possibilities for human progress which this throws up is one of the strongest arguments for liberty, and one of the weightiest cases against the attempt to reduce human society to central planning and control. As Hayek puts the case against the inhibiting influence of the planners:

If the human intellect is allowed to impose a preconceived pattern on society, if our powers of reasoning are allowed to lay claim to a monopoly of creative effort . . . then we must not be surprised if society, as such, ceases to function as a creative force.[22]

The essential point is that freedom allows people to conduct their own experiments, to make guesses about what will work or be of value to them, and to try out new ideas. We are not wise enough to know in advance what new ideas or arrangements will work in the future, and so we trust the independent and competitive efforts of many people to induce the emergence of new developments. There is no person (central planner or otherwise) who is indisputably best equipped to come up with new ideas that will prove useful. We allow everyone to make their own experiments, and take their own risks, and the ideas which prove useful will be adopted. We do not *command* progress, we *encourage its growth*.[23]

Complexity needs freedom: Hayek has neatly reversed the argument which says that we must abandon liberty because society is now so complex that it must be planned. As we have seen, this is a complete misrepresentation, for unplanned societies are capable of much greater complexity than any planned organisation. This is a subject which will be treated in more depth when we consider Hayek's views on the arguments for planning.[24]

Hayek's thoroughgoing view of liberty: Having justified liberty because it throws up undesigned novelties and improvements, Hayek says that it would not work if we restricted freedom to those cases where we *knew in advance* that its effects would be beneficial. It is not developments that can be predicted which are the objectives of freedom, but developments which are novel and unforeseen.

Freedom may be used in a variety of ways, and of course it may happen that it is used to develop things which most people might disapprove of, or that it allows actions which would shock the majority. But we do not support it nor reject it because of any particular outcome it produces; we support it because, in the long run, it has clear and obvious advantages. In Hayek's words:

Our faith in freedom does not rest on the foreseeable results in particular circumstances but on the belief that it will, on balance, release more forces for the good than for the bad.[25]

It also follows that freedom should not be limited to the amount which most people are likely to make use of. The fact that only one person in a million really wishes for the freedom to do a particular thing is no case for stopping him, because his freedom to do that particular thing might bring lasting benefits and prove of great value to us all.

Hayek's view of liberty is therefore a very thoroughgoing and even dogmatic one, for he believes that any *less* thorough defence of liberty would expose its very foundations to attack. But this is not to suggest that we can escape without any threat of coercion at all. Coercion, that is the forcing of an individual to serve the ends of another by threatening him with greater evils, cannot be avoided altogether, because the only way to prevent coercion is by the threat of coercion against those who attempt it.[26] Thus in the free society some sort of coercive apparatus is needed if coercion is, in fact, to be kept to a minimum. Free societies have usually overcome this problem by conferring a monopoly of coercion on the state, and restricting its use to that allowed by general rules.

Without the coercive apparatus of the state, it would be possible for private individuals to coerce others by the threat of violence or blackmail, and to engage in activities such as robbery, deception and fraud, all of which clearly have harmful effects on the community. The coercive power that a free society needs in this respect is not the power to make people act in particular ways, but the power to prevent its citizens from breaking the rules and to stop them engaging in these sorts of activities. Only those who break the rules are subject to coercion, and people are left free within the limits of rule-guided behaviour.

Yet there may be occasions when we want people not just to *avoid* harmful actions, but when we want them to *do* specific useful things, like paying taxes or being conscripted into the forces to fight a war. So we have to ask where lies the boundary between the free society whose government can force people to perform these duties, and the clearly unfree society whose government can command their every movement in pursuit of its own objectives and arbitrary will.

The dividing line, says Hayek, is that the government of a free people must itself be governed by rules. Even where coercion cannot be avoided, its worst effects can be mitigated by confining it to the enforcement of limited and foreseeable duties. If we know what actions are expected of us, in terms of things we *must not* do and things we *must* do, and know the rules which bind the government in its use of force, then at least we are spared the arbitrary nature of many governments. For Hayek, then, the free society is not one which is without rules or laws or government powers, but it is one in which government itself is limited by predictable rules.[27] To discover what laws and powers should exist in a free society is the central aim of most of Hayek's later writings.

THE LEGAL FRAMEWORK OF A FREE SOCIETY

Present-day thinking about the nature of the law and the purposes which a legal system ought to serve is very confused. Hayek believes that modern laws and principles of justice have grown out of the systems of rules which have long guided society and made social life possible. If we understand the nature and evolutionary function of these rule systems, therefore, we will gain a better appreciation of what the law really is and what it ought to be trying to do.

One of the sources of confusion today is that we tend to think of *any* measure passed by an elected assembly as being a 'law'. But Hayek urges us to distinguish between two very different kinds of lawmaking which are confused in the same word.[28] The first kind of law probably accounts for the bulk of measures passed by elected authorities today, and they are administrative or organisational measures. They are designed to run the machinery of government, to tell civil servants how to act, to state the purposes for which public money is to be spent, and so on. We can think of them as *commands* to government bureaucracies, telling them how to run the public sector. In a collectivist economy, all law is of this kind. The collectivist government aims at a particular outcome of social and economic affairs, the realisation of definite plans. To achieve these purposes, it *commands* its citizens how to act, and guides their behaviour towards its aims. Such a society is not based on general rules, but on the dictates of the autorities, which can be quite arbitrary and may treat individuals very inconsistently.

The law of a free society: A free society, however, is not commanded by those in authority but rests on its members' acceptance of general rules of action and their prevailing opinion of what actions are just or unjust. It is from this system of general rules, says Hayek, that the law in its true sense grows. For the law in this sense is not about commands for the administration of government, but about the discovery and determination of the rules of just conduct.

We can imagine how the law might have grown since prehistoric times. For millenia during his early development, man probably lived in small tribal groups. The headman of such a community would have two important functions. The first would be to issue *commands* about what specific activities the group should engage in and how these objectives should be achieved. The second would be to *judge* between members of the group in cases of dispute between them. It is this activity which leads to a gradual understanding of the principles of justice and eventually to their being written down as laws in the true sense.

What the headman would be faced with is a community which is largely based on the observance of rules of behaviour: taboos against certain kinds of actions, and established ways of treating and not treating other people in the group. These are not rules which the headman would have any power to change. On the contrary, they are rules which would be regarded as established, simply 'given' and obvious. The task of the headman would be to teach and enforce this *accepted framework* of general rules.

As societies grew and relied less on commands and more on general rules, this judicial function of the headman or main

29

authority would increase. Cases of dispute would arise, and judgements would have to be given more and more. The attempt to justify any such judgement would lead to the attempt to express the rules in words. So where before the rules were simply obvious, now people attempt to express more precisely what they really are. The aim of the articulation of the rules is not to invent new ones, but to be clear about how the established rules actually apply in difficult cases.

This process of gradually expressing in words what had long been the established practice must have been a long and difficult one, needing frequent restatement of the rules as new test cases challenged the existing verbal formulations.[29] Yet it was the origin of the complex principles of law which we have today. It was (and continues to be) a continuing attempt to crystallise our intuitive and unspoken sense of what is just and unjust into more accurate statements. The function of the headman of the past or the judge of today is therefore not to *create* new laws, but to *discover* what the rules of justice really are.

The rules which the judge tries to discover are therefore in a very important sense independent of headmen, governments or judges.[30] They are the product of the evolutionary selection of different groups of men with different systems of rules, and exist because they help particular groups to survive and prosper better than others, not because they have been decreed by anyone. The judge has to attempt to discover what the rules are and to refine our ideas of them when these are inadequate. Where the rules appear to conflict, he will have to decide which should prevail in the case concerned. But his hands are not completely free, because the rules he is dealing with all have an impact on the functioning of the overall social order. As Hayek puts it:

Those rules of just conduct have therefore a 'meaning' or 'function' which no one has given them. . . . [31]

The judge therefore has to decide cases against this background of accepted rules which have important social functions. He cannot simply propose new rules, because he has no way of telling whether these might be harmful to the working of the overall order. And when he proposes a refinement of an existing rule, he has to take into account the other rules already in operation, and the effect it might have overall.

The rule of law: Having separated true law, which is discovered, from commands, which are decided upon arbitrarily by government authorities, we can now understand Hayek's prescription for keeping coercion to a minimum. Since the monopoly on coercion is to be in the hands of the government (in order to prevent its use by others), it is important that this immense power should not be misused. Government must therefore itself be constrained by general rules, what Hayek calls the *rule of law*.

Hayek's doctrine of the rule of law does not tell us what particular laws there ought to be, or what particular sorts of behaviour ought to be subject to legal restraints. He is not suggesting a body of law that we should adopt. He is giving us a 'meta-legal' doctrine, a set of standards against which we can judge any laws, regardless of their particular content, to see whether they can be considered as true laws and part of the rule of law, or whether they are mere arbitrary commands. These are summarised below.

What distinguishes the free from the unfree society is that in the former each individual has a recognised and extensive private sphere, a protected domain into which government authority cannot intrude.[32] In a free society, an individual cannot be ordered about, but is expected to obey only the accepted rules, usually rules which *prohibit* certain actions rather than *demand* them, and which are applicable to all. There must be no possibility that the laws can lose their foundation in common opinion of what is just, reflected in the accepted ways of acting.

And thus we can see the next standard by which Hayek would judge any law. It must not try to order about any particular individual or group or persons, nor discriminate in favour of any identifiable person or group, or against any identifiable person or group. All laws should thus apply equally to everyone, and even to unknown people who might come along in the future.[33]

The next characteristic of laws is that they must be *known and*

31

certain. Complete certainty of the law is, of course, an ideal which we can never attain, since we are constantly refining the verbal formulations of law which we make in our continuing attempts to discover the rules of true justice. These formulations, however, must always be consistent with accepted notions of the 'sense of justice' and thus make it possible to predict with some accuracy the outcome of any court case in which they are tested.

In order to be known and certain, it is of course important that laws should never be retroactive in their effect, because then no individual would ever have a means of predicting how they would affect him, nor what behaviour he should avoid in order to keep within the retroactive laws of the future.

Socialism and the rule of law: Many institutions, such as the right of *habeus corpus* and to trial by jury, might be important procedural safeguards of individual liberty. Yet even with these institutions it is unlikely, says Hayek, that liberty could be protected without the basic acceptance and belief in some abstract rules of law which bind all authority.[34] Under the rule of law, everybody is bound by rules, including the government.

The rule of law therefore ensures that decisions are made according to known and general rules and not according to the apparent desirability of particular outcomes. The role of a judge is to assist the process of selection of general rules by upholding those which have worked well, and to improve the certainty of the law. He decides a dispute in terms of the existing, general laws. If he cast aside these general rules and decided cases according to what outcome he preferred to see in each, or to some particular objective he was trying to achieve, respect for the law would soon break down.

Hayek argues that socialist measures therefore do not pass the test of the rule of law. They are designed to bring about a particular state of affairs, to achieve an object or communal plan. As such, they necessarily mean an intrusion into the private sphere of the individual, for they will be commands which arrange people into a particular social organisation, not general rules applying to everyone. In a society of individuals who are all different, for example, any socialist measure which intended to make them equal would require treating them unequally.

The rule of law fixes only the rules for the social game. It does not attempt to specify who will be winners or losers, or what the society produced by these rules will look like. We adhere to the rules because they produce an overall order, but we do not know exactly how they do it, because the large, complex society of which we are a part has grown without being consciously designed, and because the millions of individuals and specific events which determine the outcome are themselves very complex and unpredictable. But the socialist is aiming at a particular overall order, and so he has to make people his tools and constrain them to act in particular ways, treating them differently as he deems necessary in an attempt to establish the overall utopian objective. His powers must not be limited, since only the outcome is important to him. It is, in short, the very antithesis of the rule of law.

CHANGE AND DEVELOPMENT OF THE RULES

Hayek reminds us that it is dangerous to abandon all our traditional rules and values and to attempt to re-cast society from scratch, because social institutions contain a 'knowledge' or 'wisdom' of which we are only dimly aware. But he is at pains not to suggest that our rules and values must remain static, or that it is never possible to criticise them; indeed, he offers us a mechanism under which the rules of an unplanned, spontaneous, 'grown' society can and do change.[35]

The evolution of a social system which is based on the general observance of rules by individuals naturally requires that it is possible to have some gradual improvement and change of the rules themselves, says Hayek. But consistency must be the basic test. We check what actions seem to be permissible under some general rule by seeing how it applies in new and unforeseen circumstances; we see whether a rule is self-contradictory in some cases; and, most important, we have to abandon some rules and sacrifice some moral values if they prove to be in conflict with other rules and values which we think are more important. We are therefore always evaluating the rules; but we do so against the *background* of existing rules. A rule or value is judged by how well it fits in with all the others, most of which are unquestioned; so if there appears to be an inconsistency, there is often only one decision we can make. It should be noted that we adjust our rules when they are inconsistent, and that we can never assess them out of the context of our traditional and accepted values. In Hayek's view it is an illusion to suggest that human reason is so powerful that it allows us to soar above our civilisation and to judge our rules and values in some 'scientific' or objective way, and that we can produce a better civilisation by completely redesigning them. All we can do is to confront some rules of civilisation with other parts, and decide which we prefer. This is so because our reason is not something which is outside society or free from human values; our minds have themselves evolved as part of human civilisation. We did not and cannot design society. We are certainly not intelligent enough for that.

Science and social science, of course, do have an important place in the selection of rules and values. Increases in our knowledge allow us to make better judgements about which rules we should retain and which we should abandon as inconsistent. The discovery of the evolutionary function of our rules is particularly important. But we should always remember that our knowledge of social structures is limited, and we should not make 'scientific' judgements about society on the basis of knowledge which we do not in fact possess.

Emergence of the great society: Hayek is of the opinion that the change in human rules and values which made it possible to move from a small hunting community to the modern commercial society of today must have been a major one, occupying many centuries and causing much turmoil. Yet it is instructive to reconstruct the process and look at how the rules actually changed.[36]

One can imagine the small tribal community of a few thousand years ago, similar to the communities which still exist in remote parts of the world. These groups would be of perhaps forty persons, led by a headman, pursuing a hunter-gatherer way of life, and defending their territory against all outsiders.

Each band would be regulated by its own rules, probably enshrined in ritual and magic. Some values, such as sharing of food and other resources, and even the presence of a ranking order of individuals, were instinctive, while others, perhaps marriage customs, might have emerged in evolution. The individuals in the group would adhere to them all, however, not because they understood their origin or social significance, but because the groups which acted on them prospered and grew.

It would be impossible to recount all the various changes in these rules which allowed human society to expand beyond the hunting band and into the vast societies of today. But we can be sure that it was the relaxation of some rules, probably those which were thought to be least essential, that led to it. Such change was possible because, as today, some rules bind us less strongly than others, and the flouting of some traditional values is looked upon less gravely than others; so there is always scope for change. One can imagine that bartering with other communities arose in the tribal state, for example. This would lead to a recognition of private property, and to contractual obligations between people (instead of the mere arbitrary fiat of the headman). Rates of exchange for bartered products would lead to an appreciation of relative prices and the establishment of markets.

Such changes in behaviour, due initially to the flouting of the weaker rules, brought about a major change in social organisation. None of our ancestors could have known that bartering and the protection of property and contracts would lead ultimately to the division of labour, specialised trades and the formation of large impersonal markets.[37]

And, of course, it would be impossible to return, because the rules of social organisation in the large, extended society of today (which Hayek calls the 'Great Society')[38] have allowed so great a growth in human population. To abandon those rules and return to reliance on tribal instincts would spell disaster. Yet this is precisely what many utopian social reformers would wish on us. By arguing that society should be controlled centrally, as if by a headman, and that its products should be shared or that private property should be abolished, they do not realise that:

35

Socialism is simply a re-assertion of that tribal ethics whose gradual weakening had made an approach to the Great Society possible.[39]

Such ethics may work in the small society where everyone knows everyone else, but in the large society of today, where we do not even know the people we co-operate and trade with, we must be governed not by tribal instincts but by general rules. Hayek expresses it thus:

In the small group the individual can know the effects of his actions on his several fellows, and the rules may effectively forbid him to harm them in any manner and even require him to assist them in specific ways. In the Great Society many of the effects of a person's actions on various fellows must be unknown to him. It can, therefore, not be the specific effects in the particular case, but only rules which define kinds of actions prohibited or required, which must serve as guides to the individual.[40]

THE EVOLUTION OF MODERN SOCIETY

Hayek's attempt to understand the nature of the development from the ethics of the small hunting band to the elaborate rules of the extended modern society is central to his later writings. *The Fatal Conceit* is largely an effort to explain the evolutionary processes which have made socialism out of date and inappropriate in the vast, impersonal societies of today. The analysis is difficult, but very rewarding for the reader.

Hayek is in no doubt that the change from the socialistic ethics of the tribal band to the ethics appropriate for today is indeed a very great one. He likens it to the evolutionary development of the sense of sight. This sense enabled animals, for the first time, to respond to events at a distance. Likewise, the development of the rules of the Great Society allowed individuals to adjust their behaviour quickly and effectively to the behaviour of others whom they did not even know. In the tribal group, our actions could be specifically tailored to serve the needs of people we could see; in the modern social order, we follow general rules which benefit not only ourselves but also countless others we may never meet.

But this elaborate network of rules is not of our own design:

we were not intelligent enough to see its benefits in advance. It has simply grown and evolved. Groups which adopted particular sets of rules flourished and spread, and their systems of rules spread with them. Those who could develop restraints upon their old tribal morality, deeply ingrained in their instincts as it was, could form larger societies which were not dependent on each member knowing the others personally. They could grow in number, and the rules could spread with them.

In a sense, man was civilised against his wishes. The old morality was deeply embedded in human instincts as a result of the hundreds of millenia which men spent in tribal groups. It is only by acquiring restraints upon these tribal instincts that we can hope to develop from such groups; and because they often conflict with our embedded emotions, we often rebel against these new restraints and yearn for the easy socialism of the past.

The nature of the new morality: What, then, were the main features of the new morality which enabled us to move out of the primitive group and to form what Hayek's later works call 'the extended order'? There are, he says, three very important institutions which probably formed the spine of the new order: the rules of private property, honesty, and the institution of the family.

It did not require human beings to be aware of the great benefits which these institutions bring for them to flourish. Just by adopting them, their practitioners gained an edge in the struggle for survival, and so the institutions were preserved and spread. We owe our civilisation to institutions which we did not understand, and rules of whose ultimate benefits we were not aware, but rules and institutions which survived nonetheless.

In taking the example of the institution of private property, it is easy to see how its adoption would benefit a particular group. The rules of exchange of property would allow bartering and enable the wants of others to be anticipated and provided for in exchange for other goods or services. They provide the greatest benefit, as we will see, when the needs of the two sides are most diverse. The division of labour, whereby individuals provide very specific services, is then only a step away. This in turn enables much higher levels of productivity to be achieved than if everyone tried to be self-sufficient. This prosperity enables human numbers to be expanded, with yet more specialisation, yet more productivity, and yet more population growth.

The natural history of religion: There is an interesting sidelight to Hayek's story of human development. We have seen that many parts of the new morality would be in conflict with our inherited instincts and so would be difficult to perpetuate. Hayek speculates that the new rules were often enshrined in elaborate taboos and religions, the rigid application of which enabled the rules themselves to survive. Once again, this development was not planned; it just happened to succeed.

Religion has therefore played a very important role in the development of humankind from the primitive to the modern society. And it is interesting that, while new religions come and go, the only religions which persist for any length of time are those which reinforce the new morality. That is, the only durable religions are those which enshrine the institutions of private property, honesty and the family.

Hayek cannot resist the impish suggestion that communism is a recent form of religion, one which tries to reassert our instinctive values and rejects the values of the modern social order. But its condemnation of the family and, in particular, of private property has mitigated against it, and the workings of cultural evolution are today in the process of disposing of the doctrine, yet another mistaken guess on the long road of human progress.

A self-regulating mechanism: The fact that modern institutions have prompted such rapid population growth may be bad news to those who fear a population explosion; but Hayek argues that this fear is mistaken, for the processes which have caused the increase in population also control it.

It is an interesting fact that economic advance has its greatest effect at what Hayek calls the 'periphery' of development. In the highly developed countries, those which used to be called the capitalist or market economy countries, people no longer use their extra wealth to produce larger families. Extra wealth produces the greatest benefits among the very poor, because it allows people to survive who would formerly have lacked the resources to do so.

One sees this in the shanty-towns which can be found around many rapidly growing cities. These towns do not represent a proletariat suppressed by capitalism; they represent individuals who, under any system other than capitalism, would not be alive at all, because only capitalism can generate the resources to sustain them.

And it is no accident that this proliferation of poor people is most commonly found where East meets West, at the margin between the societies based on primitive group morality and those based on modern rule-guided morality. In the primitive group, extra wealth is used to create larger families, and so improve the prospects of group survival; many of those who live beside, and rely on the benefits of, modern capitalist cities are still not fully accommodated into the new morality, which explains their large numbers and poor material conditions. But as more and more of the world is embraced by the institutions of the market economy, the margin between the old and the new must shrink. The present period of rapid multiplication of mankind will then be over, and human population levels will stabilise.

The disastrous consequences of socialism: We can therefore see how the view that we have designed the institutions of modern society and can alter them at will could prove to be such a fatal conceit. Most of those who are alive today owe their existence to the new institutions, the institutions which allowed human population to increase to about two hundred times the size it was before the dawn of modern civilisation. To abandon those institutions would consign most of humanity to starvation.

It is not surprising that many people should rebel against those institutions, such as the traditional rules of property and honesty, which sit uneasily on our comfortable ancient instincts. It is even less surprising that some men should desire to sweep away institutions whose effect we have never properly understood. Hence the error of the great revolutionary movements is not one of value, but one of fact: they presume that by deliberately organising ourselves, we can produce more, or can distribute the same amount more equally. We have, however, long outgrown the kind of society which can be supported by conscious planning.

We must now turn, therefore, to examine just how the rules of economic activity operate, and to discover how unplanned and misunderstood institutions have given rise to the boundless social orders of the modern world and have contributed to the proliferation and prosperity of humankind.

CHAPTER TWO

The Market Process

We are only beginning to understand on how subtle a communication system the functioning of an advanced industrial society is based – a communications system which we call the market and which turns out to be a more efficient mechanism for digesting dispersed information than any that man has deliberately designed.[1]

THE tendency of human beings to suppose that something which is consciously designed and planned to fulfil a certain purpose must necessarily be better than something which has grown up naturally, is nowhere more apparent than in discussions about economic activity. For it is generally agreed that most of the world's economies have developed the way they have without much conscious thought being put into their design. To many people, it therefore seems much more desirable that we should create an economy that is planned out in advance, where individuals are assigned roles as best fit their abilities and where common objectives are pursued for the benefit of all. The only alternative seems to be an economic jungle in which people are motivated more by self-interest than by common purposes or welfare.

The most powerful arguments for economic planning have always stressed this rational ordering or priorities and the organisation of individual effort for mutual advantage. By directing activities in concert, it is suggested, we can abolish the waste of unnecessary duplication, of competition and of advertising, we can all gain from the economies of scale that will be possible in large communal industries, and the most pressing social and economic objectives can be awarded the highest priorities. How can the liberal economic system ever live up to this intelligently ordered set of purposes which the planned economy boasts?

RECIPROCAL, NOT COMMON PURPOSES

Hayek's answer to this challenge is that the market order is superior precisely *because* it does not require agreement on what aims are to be pursued. It allows men with many different values and purposes to live together peacefully and to their mutual benefit, because in following their own interests, each will further the aims of many others with different and possibly conflicting interests.[2]

This is perhaps a remarkable conclusion, and to understand it properly we must recognise the special attributes of the market order. The workings of the marketplace are certainly structured and orderly, with transactions being conducted according to customary rules of property and contract, and they produce a recognisable overall order or pattern. But the pattern of activity produced by the market process is not the creation of any conscious design or planning. There is no single aim or purpose to it, for it is the outcome of many people pursuing their own individual aims and purposes. The market order therefore is not, nor ever could be, governed by any single scale of values or hierarchy of objectives like a planned economy, but serves the separate and diverse ends of all its individual members.[3]

Benefits of voluntary exchange: That the market order is not guided by any unitary system of purposes is thought to be its major defect by many critics. This stems from the belief that if the actions of individuals are not linked by common objectives, they must necessarily be unco-ordinated, wasteful and even mutually destructive. But it is, on the contrary, the greatest benefit of the market order that it enables men to live together and benefit each other *even though* they may be unable to agree on common purposes.

Consider the simplest kind of market exchange, that of the bartering of goods between two individuals, something which probably started between human tribal societies long ago. In Hayek's view, while the small tribal groups probably shared all their resources within each group (a strong instinctive urge), they no doubt found that they could derive benefits from exchanging things with others. This could be because each had an excess of something the other needed, or it could be due to the simple but useful fact that different people often have different uses for the same things. It could not have been long before men, even enemies, were enjoying the great benefits that arose from widespread trade. And, significantly, these benefits were possible even though the two parties to the exchange might have had quite diverse purposes. In fact, *the greater the differences* in the needs and purposes of each, *the more likely* it would be that they would gain from the transaction! All that they would need for both to benefit were some accepted rules (perhaps not even spoken, but generally understood) about the ownership of the commodities traded and how these could be exchanged by consent.

Little has changed today, even though the number of individuals in the marketplace has increased from two to many millions, and though we no longer trade only with people we meet, but indirectly, through the medium of money, with people we do not know and may never meet. Still our purposes co-ordinate, though they are not identical. An individual might supply a product to another, and gain from the exchange, even though he might thoroughly disapprove of the purposes of the buyer if he knew them, and though the buyer might disapprove of his. But this is the great source of strength of the market order; it allows people to co-operate even though they do not share common aims, and it makes people into partners who might otherwise be enemies fighting over the same resources.

Economic interdependence: Of course there are many individuals and organisations working in a strictly non-economic sense to resolve the differences between people, particularly to ease the differences between nations. But it is to the credit of the market order that it already enables the co-operation of individuals to occur throughout the globe, whatever divergent opinions continue to exist. Hayek puts it so:

That interdependence of all men, which is now in everybody's mouth and which tends to make all mankind One World, not only is the effect of the market order but could not have been brought about by any other means. What today connects the life of any European or

American with what happens in Australia, Japan or Zaire are repercussions transmitted by the network of market relations.[4]

It would be a pious hope to suppose that any collection of nations, indeed anything other than rather small groups of people, could agree on a common system of economic targets. The call for central planning seems to fall at the first hurdle. But, fortunately, it is not *ends* which bind people. The relations between men are really *means-relations*, allowing the reconciliation of diverse purposes, the bringing together of people with very different beliefs and objectives because they all benefit from the arrangement. Hayek regrets that many people are unwilling to accept that the unity of mankind depends ultimately on the economic relations between them, and on their pursuit of private satisfaction. But it does.

The limits of economic policy: We see, then, that the market order is something very different from a tool which is purposefully made to serve chosen ends. The market order merely reconciles competing purposes, serving all of them but not giving any guarantees about which will be satisfied first, for in such a system there does not exist any single scale of values. Since it does not 'aim' at any particular objectives, we cannot criticise it if some particular value that might be named is not in fact achieved by it. Its effect (for the phrase 'its purpose' would be inappropriate) is to increase the possibility of all of us achieving our own aims. To attempt to direct it otherwise would change its entire nature and destroy the benefits we enjoy as a result of it.

If there is a role for policy in such an order, as Hayek insists there is, it must attempt to increase the chances of all the unknown individuals in the market achieving their similarly unknown purposes. The benefits of the market order stem from millions of individuals being able to pursue their own individual objectives, and require that we do not attempt to control the order or degree to which these various needs will be met. The object of public policy in a free society will, therefore, not be an attempt to impose a single scale of values and purposes on this order, but to allow the great variety of individual purposes to be achieved. Since we could never know everybody's changing needs and the best way of achieving them at any moment, our policy must allow them to use the operation of the market as freely as possible.[5]

THE TELECOMMUNICATIONS SYSTEM OF THE MARKET

We now have to ask how it is that the market seems to be able to satisfy millions of individual purposes and to reconcile the diverse aims and activities of many people without requiring any conscious planning or control. Many people are confused on this point because they still think of 'the economy' as something deliberately fashioned for known objectives, as we would fashion a tool or organise an army to fight a battle. Hayek suggests a better analogy: the market system is more like a 'game' of exchange. It is a wealth-creating game, where all the players benefit from their involvement, although they all have their own goals. And like a game, the outcome depends on a mixture of skill and luck.

What goals will be achieved first, and to what degree each player will benefit from the game of wealth-creation is, of course, unknown at the beginning. As in a competitive sport, it is only a measure of doubt about the outcome which makes the activity interesting and worthwhile, stimulating people to take risks and make efforts which, in the market system, benefit others as well. It would be pointless to play a game where we knew the results in advance; the most we can do is set the rules fairly so that there is an equal chance for everyone to benefit and to make such efforts as they deem worthwhile. As in any game, the rules governing market exchange must not aim at improving the chances of any individual or aim at any overall pattern of results, but should treat everyone equally and maximise the chances of any one of them, picked at random, deriving benefits from the exchange process itself.

The market order is not like an ordinary board game, however, because there are many contributing players, most of whom are completely unknown to the others. Clearly, therefore, it requires a very sophisticated system of communications if they are to be part of the 'game' of the market order at all. We are indeed fortunate, argues Hayek, that the market system provides us with a remarkably comprehensive communications network: the network of *prices*. The rewards to each player in the game depend upon the prices at which he can sell his product in the market. And in turn (although he does not need to know it) those prices will reflect the strength of the needs which others have for that product. Prices therefore act as signals which enable an individual, unknowingly, to contribute to the satisfaction of the needs of other people as the same time as he strives for the satisfaction of his own. As an example, Hayek suggests:

The manufacturer does not produce shoes because he knows that Jones needs them. He produces because he knows that dozens of traders will buy certain numbers at various prices because they (or rather the retailer they serve) know that thousands of Joneses, whom the manufacturer does not know, want to buy them.[6]

The determination of prices: Some simple illustrations are provided in Hayek's various writings which demonstrate how the commonplace action of the price system transmits the most sophisticated information throughout the market. Suppose, for example, that a new use for some resource such as tin has been discovered, or that an existing source of tin has become exhausted.[7] Significantly, it does not matter to the trader which of these two causes has occurred. All he needs to know is that he must economise on tin because it now commands a higher price; the change in market conditions has enabled tin producers to obtain more for their product. Some users of tin will no doubt economise, perhaps switching to substitute materials that are now cheaper. Thus the scarce tin will continue to be employed only where alternatives are unavailable or are more expensive. The new demand for substitutes will prompt *their* further supply or switching from less profitable employments, which will in turn affect the things which can be substituted for the substitutes, and so on. The entire market order adjusts to the scarcity or new demand for tin, and acts as one market, even though few people were aware of the original cause of the changes. Users and producers do not need to scan the whole field, or be aware of the various uses for tin and its substitutes, for this adjustment to occur and for the relevant information to be communicated to all. The local prices of these goods are all they need to know in order for a complete adjustment to be made.

The most remarkable fact about prices, in Hayek's view, is that in this way they can match the purposes of many unknown people by summarising a great deal of information very simply. Any central economic planner would need to know all of the various uses and end purposes for tin and its substitutes before he could even *begin* to work out what switching should occur, but the market provides the adjustment rapidly and without any need to find out all this detailed personal information. Hayek says of the price system that:

In abbreviated form, by a kind of symbol, only the most essential information is passed on and passed on only to those concerned. It is more than a metaphor to describe the price system as a kind of machinery for registering change, or a system of telecommunications which enables individual producers to watch merely the movement of a few pointers, as an engineer might watch the hands of a few dials, in order to adjust their activities to changes of which they may never know more than is reflected in the price movement.[8]

The use of local information: Thus the price system, with the minimum of effort being required, tells individuals in the marketplace about the range of wants which others have, and the extent to which they desire those wants to be satisfied. But there is an even more subtle aspect to the information which the market system can convey to others and therefore make use of. This is the special knowledge of time and place which individuals possess.

There is a tendency to think of human knowledge as a single whole, a collection of information which is available to all. But in fact most of the knowledge of the world is not accessible to others, and some of the things we call 'knowledge' are really the conflicting theories of various experts: so knowledge is very far from being 'organised'. A trip through any reference and research library would confirm Hayek's point; although much 'knowledge' is concentrated in a single spot, it is doubtful that any one mind could scan it all or understand but a fragment of it, and even a computer would be unable to resolve its conflicting opinions and use it as the basis for rational planning. And, more important still, there is a great deal of human knowledge which cannot be written down in books or summarised in statistics, or even communicated as quickly as it is discovered. This is knowledge of the changing circumstances of particular places and times, which only the individuals concerned can make use of.

This sort of knowledge is the knowledge possessed by the estate agent, for example. His information is about temporary opportunities in a rapidly shifting market, in which the needs of many prospective buyers, all different, have to be matched with the property which becomes available each day. The shipper who earns his living from using otherwise empty cargo vessels on their return journeys provides another example of this 'unorganised' knowledge. The foreign currency dealer who gains from the volatile differences in exchange rates between the currencies of different countries gives us a particularly plain illustration of how temporary and fleeting the opportunities may be.[9]

The telecommunications system of the market, which allows these temporary opportunities to be grasped and individual purposes that are dependent upon time and space to be reconciled, is therefore far more subtle and advanced than that of a centralised system, in which such information could not even be summarised or communicated to the central authority fast enough to act on. It therefore increases the chance of all individuals achieving their many different ends.

Prices ensure the cheapest mix of inputs: Not only does the price system allow individuals to make use of the widest sources of information. It also allows them to compare the scarcities of many different products and the strength of many different sorts of demand as if they each had a sort of giant computer. The result of this is that the price system ensures that goods are produced in the most efficient and least costly way practicable.

There are usually several, perhaps many, different ways of making the same product. The buyers of tarpaulins, for instance, are probably little concerned whether they are made from a base of hemp, flax, jute, cotton or nylon. The producer therefore chooses the material which comes at least cost – that is, the material which requires the least sacrifice of other desirable products. In aiming for the lowest cost, his actions release the maximum amount of resources which can be used for other purposes.[10]

And the advantage stretches further than this. In many cases, a product will require a mix of inputs, and almost any such product can be made with different combinations of the various inputs or their substitutes. Once again, the manufacturer will choose the least costly mix of inputs, comparing the relative prices of each factor of production. What the prices of the various inputs tell everyone is the proportion in which other manufacturers (of many different kinds of product) prefer to use one product instead of another. If any particular commodity, like tin, is worth more to an individual relative to other commodities than the market price difference between them, he can substitute more tin for other things. If it is worth less to him than the price difference, he will economise on tin and use more of the other materials which are cheaper, and so on through all the various factors of production. In changing his demand, the individual will contribute his mite of information to the price signals, and so will others, affecting all users of the products. There is therefore a tendency towards similarity in different people's rates of substitution of various goods which secures the most efficient use of resources. The price difference between two goods tends to reflect the relative worth of those goods in the minds of producers; and this is true for any pair of the millions of goods available. Each manufacturer will therefore produce his output at the least cost in terms of the products that others will, in consequence, lack and want.[11]

The price mechanism is therefore, as Hayek describes it, something of a 'marvel'.[12] Although the mechanism is blind, requiring no orders to be issued nor purposes agreed on, it directs the thousands of different available commodities into their most efficient mix of uses. It really does work as if a giant computer were calculating all the different possible mixes and substitution rates which are available; but all that manufacturers need to know is the limited information of the relative prices between any two goods.

The market achieves a true maximum: The market system does not depend on people 'working hard' but on their making the things that other people desire, in the way which conflicts least with the desires of yet others, and at the right time and in the right place to satisfy the consumers. The rewards offered by the market system are not based on any 'just' reward for effort or personal merit, nor do they always reflect the investment of resources which a manufacturer has made in bringing his product to market: often, manufacturers will be disappointed because they have overestimated the demand for their goods or have miscalculated the cost of producing them. Market rewards reflect the *value to others* of a commodity and the efforts of the individual who supplies it. They are thus an incentive to future action which will benefit others.

Some thinkers, such as Marx,[13] adopted a 'labour theory of value' which suggested that the value of a product was determined by the amount of labour invested in it (a theory used to justify the expropriation of capitalists, who do not seem to invest any labour in the production of goods and therefore presumably contribute no value to them). But this is, of course, the exact inverse of reality in Hayek's eyes. Prices inform producers how much labour and skill it is *worth putting into* a product, and any failure to understand this necessarily incapacitates one from ever understanding the function of the market.

Yet the rewards which the market offers, because they reflect the actual benefits conferred on others, do not discriminate between skill or luck in enabling the producer to have the right product at the right time. In most cases it will undoubtedly be a mixture of both. Therefore, in a society which is not planned to achieve a particular outcome, we can never predict what share of the overall rewards any particular individual will enjoy. But Hayek argues (although it may be no consolation to those at the bottom of the stack) that each share will be as large as it could be in an important sense. Since prices and competition direct resources into their most efficient uses, each individual's share of the total will be won at the lowest cost that is possible.

Hayek's conclusion on this sharing out of market rewards is as follows:

It would, of course, be unreasonable to demand more from the operation of a system in which the several actors do not serve a common hierarchy of ends but co-operate with each other only because they can thereby mutually assist each other in their respective pursuit of their individual ends. Nothing else is indeed possible in an order in which the participants are free. . .[14]

COMPETITION IN A FREE ECONOMY

The price mechanism is one of many systems which man has learnt to use (although inadequately) after he stumbled on it without understanding it. He did not design an economy and then select the price system as a way of co-ordinating it; his fortunate discovery *facilitated* the expansion of a complex and widespread economic system.[15] It made possible the use of widely dispersed knowledge, and of the division of labour which contributes so greatly to raising the efficiency of the productive process, allowing everyone to specialise in whatever manufacturing activities he excels at.

Competition between producers (and, indeed, between consumers) is another essential part of the market process, ensuring that economic information is transmitted to others through prices, and is acted upon. The old belief that competition means the duplication of similar work and is therefore 'wasteful' stems from a completely mistaken view of the nature and purposes of competition, a mistaken view which is reinforced by much traditional discussion of 'perfect competition' in economics textbooks. Hayek points out the weaknesses of the usual approach, and then offers his own view of the true nature and functions of the competitive process.[16]

The textbook view of competition: Economics textbooks usually outline the concept of 'perfect competition' at an early stage, and from the supposed advantages of this are derived the arguments of many supporters of the market, and from the supposed disadvantages of it come most of its critics. Both are wrong, in Hayek's mind, and the many advantages of competition thankfully do not rest on its being 'perfect' in any way.

51

The traditional model of perfect competition rests on foundations which do not exist except in every limited parts of economic life. The primary assumption of the model is that any well-defined product or service can be supplied to most consumers at the same cost by a large number of producers, with the result that none of them can deliberately determine the price. Any producer, runs this model, who raised his price would lose his customers, while any producer who lowered his price would face retaliatory action from his competitors. Prices are therefore as low as possible, only high enough to be just profitable (which attracts the supporters of the market), because there are many producers duplicating the production of the same good or service (which raises criticisms of its being wasteful).

The other assumptions of the perfect competition model are equally unlikely. They are the assumption of complete knowledge of all the relevant facts about the market and about the technical possibilities of the production methods available; and of the absence of barriers to entry into the production process.

Hayek's criticism: Hayek's criticism of this traditional view is not simply that it is very unlikely to occur; it is that it completely distorts the idea of competition, which is more of an *activity* than a static state of affairs. To Hayek, every economic problem arises because something *changes* – the supply of a commodity or discovery of new uses for it, for example. The study of economics is the study of how adjustments are made in this constantly moving world; and to freeze the picture at one point in time, as the traditional textbook approach does, tells us precisely nothing.

The 'perfect competition' assumption that producers possess perfect knowledge of their markets is an obvious example of this. Nobody has perfect knowledge, which is why we rely on the price system as a method – good, but undoubtedly far from perfect – for *spreading* knowledge. In Hayek's words:

It will be obvious . . . that nothing is solved when we assume everybody to know everything and that the real problem is rather how it can be brought about that as much of the available knowledge as possible is used.[17]

The theory of competitive equilibrium therefore *assumes away* something which it is the main task of the process of competition to discover. A producer could never be considered to have complete knowledge about the changing and unforeseeable costs of his inputs, and nor is the price at which he can sell a given quantity of his product known in advance. How much a consumer will buy, and at what price, depends upon the various choices which are put before him, which depend upon the activities of many suppliers of many different sorts of product and on the consumer's circumstances and tastes at the time. It is impossible for such facts of consumer choice to be 'given'; we cannot say how a consumer will react to a choice until that choice is put before him.

The assumption that any product can be fully homogeneous – that is, that consumers are completely indifferent about which source of supply they choose – is equally unlikely. The function of competition *is* to differentiate producers, to convince buyers that one is better than his competitors. No two doctors, or grocers, or travel agents, will be exactly alike, but this does not mean that there is no competition between them. Competition between non-identical firms, overlooked by the textbooks, can in fact be very fierce.

Perfect knowledge about the available methods of production and the costs of manufacture is therefore an absurd assumption. No two firms are identical: the factor mixes they deem important (including wrapping, advertising and so on) and the historical accidents of their foundation and past production will make them all different. They may share some knowledge about manufacturing, but there will always be many particular differences which will be reflected in the product they each take to the market.

This, says Hayek, is no mere verbal criticism. The false assumptions of the perfect competition analysis lead people into the most absurd conclusions. The assumptions of perfect competition, for example, often lead people to suppose that a more advantageous use of resources would be achieved if the existing (identical) products were produced by compulsory partnership instead of the 'duplication' of competition. And the assumptions lead other critics to suggest that the compulsory standardisation of slightly different products would yield further advantages. But a moment's reflection about the way in which competition actually stimulates the introduction of new products, and of the wide variety of tastes which they help producers to serve, should show the folly of such a view. After all:

It would clearly not be an improvement to build all houses exactly alike in order to create a perfect market for houses, and the same is true of most other fields where differences between the individual products prevent competition from ever being perfect.[18]

Competition as a discovery procedure: For Hayek, competition is not a state of affairs but an activity, and it is essentially a procedure which allows the discovery of the various tastes and preferences which individuals in the market order possess, and of the various mixes of inputs which will enable those demands to be met at the lowest possible cost. Because the facts of economic life are always changing, so too will the solutions which the competitive process suggests to the various producers.

It is competition which urges producers to seek out and experiment with new areas of demand, and to satisfy tastes and demands which may not have been recognised by other competitors. This is the entrepreneurial function, and it is important in bringing about new opportunities for the satisfaction of widespread desires. Knowledge is not perfect, and it may be that an entrepreneur comes across some need that people wish to be satisfied and then gears up to serving that need, or it may be that he makes a guess by bringing to market a new product that indeed turns out to be demanded. In either event, it is undoubtedly the presence of many potential competitors which stimulates him to move quickly and to exploit the new and untapped market. For if he failed, the market mechanism would induce someone else to step in and fill the gap. The successful entrepreneur will (at the outset at least) be rewarded by his being first in the marketplace, and the

depend on the plans of other people. His competitors will no doubt have proposals to exploit similar markets. The plans of his customers may be altered when new opportunities, perhaps of an entirely different kind, arise. And, certainly, the plans of other individuals are known only to themselves: people change their plans from time to time and may even be unaware of exactly what their plans are or how they would respond to new opportunities that might arise in the future. So it would clearly be impossible to collect this information centrally. The traditional equilibrium theory assumes that the economy is static, that it has been frozen at one moment and will continue as it is. But perfect foresight concerning what will happen is far from reality, since individuals are always at the mercy of the changing plans of others.

If there is a meaning for the word 'equilibrium', says Hayek, it is only in the context of a single individual who knows exactly what his plans will be and whose various purposes are in complete and unshakable harmony. But it can never occur in society as a whole. The plans of millions of individuals cannot be in perfect harmony because nobody knows the basis on which other people will take decisions in the future.

Yet Hayek does not reject the idea of equilibrium entirely, even though he rejects its possible use as the basis for rational economic planning. There is, he argues, a sense in which a market can loosely be said to be in equilibrium. Undoubtedly, the actions and plans of the various individuals in the marketplace do have a tendency to be reconciled with one another over time. If there is any equilibrium in the market system, it is limited to what we might call a *dynamic equilibrium*, like a stream running downhill, where currents and eddies form from time to time, but where the water tends to flow in the same overall direction. When we understand that the market order is not static, that people's reactions to new changes cannot be predicted, and that there exists no equilibrium but only a *process towards equilibrium* that is changing constantly, then we can begin to understand the futility of supposing that this complex process can be arrested, harnessed and planned.

HAYEK ON MONEY AND INFLATION

A particular case which demonstrates the importance of recognising the dynamic nature of economic adjustment is afforded by the effects of money and inflation on production. This is a problem to which Hayek devoted most of his formative years as a professional economist and is therefore of some interest. Although the nature of the problem has changed much since the early 1930s when Hayek first tackled it, his analysis continues to be relevant and the policy implications which it harbours are still momentous.[20]

Hayek and the monetarists agree that inflation is caused by an increase in the supply of money or credit in the economic system. When he was first writing in the 1930s, of course, there was much less opportunity for monetary expansion than there is today, because of the linking of the major currencies to the gold standard for most of the first half of the century. Today, there is comparatively little restraint upon the amount of currency which governments can print, or the size of credit extensions they can grant to themselves and to private industry, and this has made the problem of inflation even more acute.

But however the extra increase in credit is engineered, it shows itself in the cost of borrowing becoming lower and bank credit becoming more freely available. The people who borrow at such a time are, of course, those who expect to make a greater return on their borrowed money than it costs them to pay off the interest charges. The cheaper borrowing allows people to start up new businesses, and it allows people who already manufacture to spend more on capital equipment. The cheapness of capital investment causes what modern economists would call a deepening of the capital structure. It now becomes profitable to manufacture goods of greater complexity or refinement, requiring additional stages of production. For example, better finishing, more elaborate packaging and more extensive distribution might now be justified.

The result is that the credit expansion has caused a marked change in the distribution and use of economic resources. Hayek rather confusingly talks about 'longer production processes', yet what he means is not that production necessarily takes more time in the world of plentiful and cheap credit, but that there tend to be more elaborations and more stages in the production processes. The credit expansion leads manufacturers to order and install completely new machinery aimed at achieving these extra refinements of their products, or even to produce goods which were previously unavailable or home-made. Everyone – particularly those who manufacture the new capital equipment itself – experiences a boom.

Unfortunately, however, the manufacturing investors have responded to what Hayek calls a 'false signal'. They assumed that the falling costs of capital reflected a fairly permanent increase in the availability of money for investment. But in fact it was only a single and momentary expansion and so manufacturers find that the supply of investment funds dries up as banks run out of further credit, and as investors find it too risky to go on lending. A number of manufacturers will now find that they cannot afford some of the new production processes they had planned, and will have to abandon half-completed capital equipment or cancel their orders for new machinery and factory space. Furthermore, the money which has been spent on new capital so far will now be in the pockets of the men who built it, stimulating the demand for finished goods. Profitability will now lie not in more capital-intensive and elaborate production processes, but in shorter and less capital-intensive processes which get goods quickly to market in order to satisfy the consumers' demand.

As the original injection of money washes out of the demand for productive machinery and into people's pockets, therefore, the downward phase of the trade cycle has begun. All available resources must be switched back into producing goods quickly. Some of the elaborations in production processes must be cut out. New machinery which cannot be used for other purposes will be abandoned. Producers of capital equipment will find a sudden drop in the demand for their products and will have to cut back in investment and employment. After the initial boom, in other words, there will be a slump, with men and machinery lying idle. The original monetary injection has caused not a lasting boom, but a painful slump. It is a slump which cannot be avoided if manufacturing processes are to be re-adjusted in line with economic reality: but it is a slump which is much better avoided.

The initial injection of money into the economy produces what seem to be beneficial effects. At first, almost everything succeeds when money is more plentiful: new businesses are formed and old ones re-equip. But inflation carries the seeds of its own destruction, according to Hayek. For the initial monetary boost encourages the laying down of investments which cannot be profitable in the long term because they are a response to a false signal, an artifical and fleeting demand. And this is the great difficulty with a policy of deliberate inflation: the new processes and the new jobs it creates can only be sustained in expansionary circumstances. They are due to the pull which the *change* in the money supply exerts. Consequently, they can only last as long as the additions to the supply of money grow. To achieve the same stimulating effect, it is therefore necessary to administer *increasing doses* of inflation. As soon as the inflation ceases to accelerate, businesses at the margin must begin to fail.

Inflation causes economic dislocation: The most important feature of Hayek's analysis of money in the economy is that it is not neutral. An increase in the supply of money produces real changes in the employment of people and capital. An inflation shifts people and capital into employments which are only visible as long as the inflation continues upward.

One of the greatest oversights of the more simplistic versions of the quantity theory of money is that they overlook this important structural change which inflation causes. The elementary quantity theory suggests that an increase in the quantity of money causes, after a long and variable lag, an equivalent change in the general price level. But to talk about the 'general price level' is, in Hayek's view, only to disguise how inflation works to dislocate economic activity.[21] And it allows critics to suppose that unemployment is not a necessary consequence (sooner or later) of inflation.

Nevertheless, says Hayek, there is certainly an element of truth in the simple faith of monetarism:

... it would be one of the worst things which would befall us if the general public should ever again cease to believe in the elementary propositions of the quantity theory.[22]

But there is much more to inflation than the elementary proposition that more money causes higher prices. It is, says Hayek, *relative* prices which are crucial, because what happens to the economy depends on the point at which the money enters. If money enters at a certain point, say in a certain industry, it attracts resources and investment to that point, bidding up the relative prices of goods and productive factors associated with that industry. The relative price effects will then spread to subsidiary industries, and so on outwards, like ripples on a pool spreading away from the centre.

Or perhaps a better example provided by Hayek is that of honey being poured into a jar. Because of its stickiness, it forms a mound in the centre from which it slowly spreads outward. It will continue to keep this height for as long as we pour – a very literal illustration of Hayek's 'fluid equilibrium' concept – but as soon as we stop or slow down, the mound in the middle begins to subside.[23]

Meanwhile, this mound of money, with the higher local prices it creates, attracts more resources into the industries at the centre. It is perhaps not surprising that the industries in the British economy (such as shipbuilding and heavy engineering) which were shored up by the expansionist policies of the 1960s and 1970s should have collapsed so remarkably when the inflation was turned off in the 1980s. Like the mound of honey, which collapses completely when the flow stops, the industries which ride highest on the inflationary crest always suffer the worst collapses when the inflation stops.

The Keynesian solution: The Keynesian solution to a slump is to boost demand through expansionary policies. Investment, argued Keynes, must be expanded in order to generate new employment and production. But as we can see from Hayek's analysis, this leads only to disaster. For it is an overinvestment in the wrong places which causes the initial boom followed by the inevitable slump. Unemployment is not caused by a *shortage* of general demand; it is caused by a *mismatch* of demand and supply. For, as Hayek noted in 1939, the employment of the various sections of industry will depend at least as much on *how* the current output of goods is produced as on *how much* is produced.[24] Reviewing the concept in the 1980s, Hayek recorded this phenomenon in the following terms:

While the possibility of selling different quantities of *one* commodity depends of course on the magnitude of the demand for it, the possibility of selling a collection of a wide variety of different commodities is not in any simple manner related to the sum of the demands for them altogether. If the composition (or distribution) of the demand for the various products is very different from that of their supply, no magnitude of total demand will assure that the market is cleared.[25]

The Keynesian cure for unemployment, a deliberate expansion in general 'investment demand', is therefore the very worst policy which could be pursued if unemployment is to be minimised, for by lumping very different things together it completely ignores the true source of the unemployment problem.

Keynes was also responsible for what Hayek calls the 'final disaster',[26] that of encouraging the belief that the *government* is the source of high or low levels of employment. In fact, says Hayek, one of the most important causes of unemployment is the tendency of *trade unions* to keep wage rates high in industries that may be getting less profitable, and to enforce traditional differentials rigidly, even though the needs of the market change daily. This obstruction of the required adjustment of relative wage levels deprives the market of the guilding influence of the price of labour, and therefore guarantees that labour will be attracted into the wrong places and will not be used in its most profitable combinations. And this mismatching of labour supply with demand is bound to ensure that the total level of employment is lower than it would otherwise be.

Wrong solutions to unemployment: Hayek is clear that certain of the customary methods of alleviating unemployment will only worsen the problem. A popular view among politicians and even some professional economists, for example, is that employment can be stimulated by a continuous but 'mild' dose of inflation. But Hayek argues that this thinking is completely wrong: there is no 'trade-off' between inflation and unemployment, because all inflation actually *generates* unemployment, so that increasing doses of inflation would be needed to keep unemployment at bay until eventually the economic system is submerged in Weimar-style hyperinflation. The reasons for this are clear if Hayek's analysis is followed.

In the first place, rising prices caused by monetary expansions are not uniform across the economy; some prices rise faster than others, depending on where the new money is injected into the economy and on the capital structure of the industries concerned. Money is not neutral: it makes prices rise at different and confusing rates, so causing a number of 'false signals' for investors. Under inflation, the investor does not know where to put his money for the highest real return, and so resources often become concentrated in sectors where there is no real profitability to justify them. Even a 'mild' inflation, if prolonged, will ensure that resources become progressively more concentrated in the wrong places. This is a waste of resources, an *underemployment* of capital and manpower which is itself a crime, and which leaves the economy less and less able to compete with other countries.

And the pressures on inflation are all upward. The initial *change* in credit levels caused the initial boom. As we have seen, it takes a maintenance of the new inflation rate to sustain the new structure of economic processes, but then we are simply left with a new (and less efficient) economic structure. To keep the stimulating effect there must be another increase in the inflation rate, thus generating more new jobs and new businesses: and another and another, until eventually we have hyperinflation.

Once a given rate of inflation comes to be expected, therefore, it no longer stimulates, because only the new (albeit false) signal of a rise in new credit will prompt further employment and investment. No 'mild' but steady inflation policy is tenable, and it is certainly no answer to unemployment. Unemployment is caused by resources being in the wrong place at the wrong time: a mismatching of productive resources with the realities of demand; and only a structural change to bring production processes in line with demand will cure it. This mismatching is not abolished by a general inflation – indeed it is cocooned by it.

Hence many economies have been cursed with the phenomenon which was never predicted in, and can never be satisfactorily explained by, Keynes's analysis: that of 'stagflation', where inflation keeps rising but unemployment rises as well. At this point, some governments have been inclined to use wage and price controls in an effort to stop rising prices.

But, says Hayek, rising prices are merely the symptom of inflation and not its cause. By preventing prices from doing their work (that of controlling and directing the use of resources by signalling to buyers and sellers), price controls simply make matters worse. Artificially low prices will inhibit production, whatever the state of the real demand; and artificially low wages will lead to the employment of people in industries where they would not be justified without the controls. Instead of curing economic ills, wage and prices controls make things worse by increasing the misallocation of resources.[27]

Hayek also doubts whether indexation of prices can have much effect. It can certainly help those worst hit by inflation, especially those on fixed incomes, such as pensioners. But it is unlikely to remedy an inflation which is caused by consumers trying to buy more than there is on the market, and demanding money wages sufficiently large to fulfil their expectations.

The solution to Keynesian inflation: Inflation which is caused by deliberate monetary expansion in an attempt to boost employment can be cured only when its nature is understood. Hayek's short way of putting it is that 'Inflation must be stopped dead'.[28]

Undoubtedly this stringent solution leads to high unemployment as the labour which has been misallocated to certain industries is shed. The longer the inflation has persisted, the greater will the misallocation be, since necessary adjustments will not have been made and these errors will have accumulated over the years. But, in Hayek's view, this unemployment is the inevitable outcome of the inflation and the seeds were inherent in it. One can either opt to remove the stimulating effect of inflation slowly (which he thinks poses political difficulties of the greatest magnitude) or one can do it quickly, and tolerate a very high rate of unemployment for a comparatively short period. For once the inflation has been squeezed out and people are assured that it will not reoccur, the foundations have been laid for a real and lasting economic boom.

The job losses and the inevitable bankruptcies will be greater in some industries than others. They will be most obvious in those industries which have benefited most from the inflation (probably those at early stages of the productive processes, machine producers and so on) and those where the activities of the trade unions have resisted wage adjustments most successfully.

The first thing required if inflation is to be overcome, then, is a functioning labour market, allowing the smooth movement of workers from the jobs where there is an excess of supply to those where there is a shortage. Without that functioning labour market, there can be no useful cost calculations in industry, and therefore no efficient use of resources. Such a market can certainly exist with strong trade unions, but it can never exist where the responsibility for unemployment is seen as that of the government, and where the unions take no responsibility for the unemployment consequences of excessive wage demands.

Resting on the inflationist assumption that the power of the government is unlimited, the beliefs that full employment can be achieved by conscious direction of demand and that any problems arising from this policy can be cured by further controls are in fact a most dismal illusion. Perhaps Hayek is warning us that it is better to keep the stable door firmly locked when he says that:

. . . inflation is probably the most important single factor in that vicious circle wherein one kind of government action makes more and more government control necessary. For this reason all those who wish to stop the drift toward increasing government control should concentrate their efforts on monetary policy.[29]

CHAPTER THREE

Hayek's Critique of Socialism

That democratic socialism, the great utopia of the last
few generations, is not only unachievable, but that to
strive for it produces something so utterly different that
few of those who now wish it would be prepared to
accept the consequences, many will not believe until
the connection has been laid bare in all its aspects.[1]

THE belief that it is possible to apply rigorous, rational
planning to the economic process *and* that it is possible to direct
this using existing or modified democratic institutions is not as
strong today as it was when Hayek wrote *The Road to Serfdom*.
Yet it continues to have some appeal, and has become
widespread among Western nations, even though the planning
which is usually proposed is not as extensive as that which was
being proposed by reformers during the early part of this
century. In 1944, Hayek was able to say with conviction that:

If it is no longer fashionable to emphasise that 'we are all socialists
now', this is so merely because the fact is too obvious.[2]

And although the 'hot socialism' of that time may have cooled
somewhat,[3] Hayek's remark is still largely applicable.

Socialism is a respectable doctrine today only because people
still believe that economic planning can be achieved within the
framework of *democratic* institutions. Pointing out examples of
where the ideals of socialism have faded into tyranny does little
to discourage the socialist, of course, who believes that such a
development is by no means inevitable, and that such examples
do not represent 'true socialism'. But Leon Trotsky was
undoubtedly telling the truth when he wrote in 1937 that
'where the sole employer is the state, opposition means death
by slow starvation. The old principle: who does not work shall
not eat, has been replaced by a new one: who does not obey
shall not eat'.[4] For Hayek's analysis shows that the acceptance

66

of the ideals of socialism and central planning makes it inevitable that a large amount of power is concentrated in the hands of the controlling authorities. These authorities have to process a mountain of economic information, too much to be handled by democratic institutions and too detailed to be covered by general rules of action. Quickly, therefore, the socialist system degenerates into one of power, personal discretion, and unequal treatment under what remains of the law.[5]

Hayek's argument is that the phenomena we see in countries where socialism or national socialist planning has been attempted *are* the outcome of the creed itself, and are not historical accidents which can be avoided in the future. Hayek does not of course accuse socialists of wishing to bring these horrors about; those who pipe us down the road to serfdom genuinely believe that it leads to a socialist utopia of abundance, equality and harmony. But, he says, their vision can only be advanced by resorting to greater and greater coercion in order to make people conform to the common plan, until at last the idealists are replaced by leaders who are not so squeamish about using this apparatus of coercion for their private ends. Thus, the socialist produces the very opposite of his intentions, and Hayek sympathises with him:

Is there a greater tragedy imaginable than that, in our endeavour consciously to shape our future in accordance with high ideals, we should in fact unwittingly produce the very opposite of what we have been striving for?[6]

Hayek's warning is to the 'democratic socialist' intellectual who believes that a moderate socialism can be achieved and made the basis of a stable society. It can not. Just as the eighteenth-century political thinker, Edmund Burke, predicted the reign of terror which would be the inevitable outcome of revolutionary stirrings in France,[7] so does Hayek demonstrate the mechanism by which the dark side of the socialist force will certainly gain the upper hand unless the socialist policies are abandoned. The fact

That socialism can be put into practice only by methods which most socialists disapprove is, of course, a lesson learned by many social reformers in the past.[8]

Hayek's contribution is to explain the mechanism by which this unfortunate result occurs.

IS PLANNING INEVITABLE?

After defining the problem, Hayek begins his critique of socialism in Chapter Four of *The Road to Serfdom*[9] by asking whether a planned economy is really as inevitable a development as most people seem to think and as socialists insist.

Proponents of planning, he contends, rarely say that it is desirable; rather, they argue, like Marx, that in the struggle to become more efficient, firms become larger and larger, and that the economic system therefore comes to be dominated by giant and powerful monopolies, or, better, to have government direction of the economy so that everyone (and not just the monopolists and their shareholders) can have a say in what is produced. The problems of capitalism therefore make planning *inevitable*.

Hayek doubted the premise of this argument, that larger firms are necessarily more efficient, and now that the age of giantism is long dead, it must be agreed that he was right. A large firm can reduce certain overheads, but suffers counterveiling costs such as a bureaucratic organisation, the inability to cater to minority tastes, and a slower response to changing demand. Today, with consumers demanding new and customised products, and with new technology rapidly making old methods and products obsolete, it is perhaps only the profusion of smaller firms which can hope to keep the customers satisfied.

And does competition fall, or is it pushed? Monopolies occur quite rarely, and where they do occur they are usually run, sanctioned or aided by the government. It is clear that:

Anyone who has observed how aspiring monopolists regularly seek and frequently obtain the assistance of the power of the state to make their control effective can have little doubt that there is nothing inevitable about this development.[10]

This conclusion is supported by the historical order in which the growth of monopoly occurs. Monopoly tends to be a characteristic of young industrial countries, usually as a result of deliberate protectionism against foreign trade. Japan might be cited as a modern example, but Hayek says that the United States, Germany and Britain pursued the same course in the last century and again when trade was poor in the 1930s.[11]

There is a great deal of muddled thinking about monopoly in any case.[12] A monopoly can, in fact, be a *desirable* result of competition, if large size allows a firm to serve its customers at the lowest price. As long as others have the opportunity to compete, and the monopoly position rests on true market service and not on a special right or privilege, we should not need to worry. And in a free economy, where concentrations of capital can be built up, size becomes the best antidote to size: whatever the power of a large firm, it can always be undermined by another of similar size.

On this point, we must also be clear that size and power are not the same thing, and it is impossible to say when a firm is 'too large' or has 'harmful power'. One firm might dominate a market, and others might follow its lead on prices, but this is no proof that a better deal for the customer would arise if the firm were broken up. Its size may allow it to manufacture more cheaply than a smaller firm. And the decision about the 'optimal size' of a firm cannot be settled by politicians or economists: only the firm itself, in testing the demand in the market, can work out its most efficient size and adjust to that level. Furthermore, it should be noted that big firms often arise without dominating single markets: the strategy of most sensible corporate planners is to diversify and spread their risks across many markets. The power of the large firm to manipulate prices is therefore often overstated.

Standardisation brings efficiency: There is another argument for planning which is almost the precise opposite of the first. This is the contention that standardisation of production, and the concentration of resources into the production of a smaller range of products, would bring greater efficiency. Competition, advertising, duplication of production processes and other 'wasteful' things, it is said, could be eliminated if products were standardised. And this, of course, would require economic planning.

Hayek has no doubt that it might well be possible to obtain temporary cost advantages from the standardisation of production. But the argument, he says, completely ignores the fact that the economic process is always moving. Standardisation may bring savings today, but it robs us of savings later on, because our technology is always improving and developing, and some production problems which are expensive today may well be solved in a few years' time. By standardising our production on the basis of *present* levels of technology and knowledge, we would just be putting all our eggs into a very old-fashioned basket. The choice, then, is between savings now and a better ability to take advantage of savings that will be possible in the future.

There is another, related argument here. We cannot predict which of today's manufactures will be around in the future. A product which seems convenient and cheap today may seem very antiquated and expensive in a short time. Similarly, some products which are almost unknown today will prove their value and be in common use in the future. So when we bind ourselves to manufacturing particular standardised products in the hope that longer production runs will make them cheaper, we have stopped dead the essential *testing process* of the market. We have made a guess about what should be produced, instead of letting people's preferences show through by market choice over the years. We have abandoned the stimulus constantly to review, refine, innovate and improve our production.

One last point is worth mention. It is certainly true that new inventions have given us very great power, but it would be foolish to use this new power to destroy liberty. Hayek therefore believes that while technological improvements do not force us towards comprehensive economic planning, they would confer an awesome power upon any central authority which controlled them, and for this reason we should be particularly cautious.

The complexity of society: Another argument voiced in favour of planning is that the modern economy is now so complicated that only central planning can solve the problem of resource allocation.

Hayek believes that it is exactly the other way around. Society and the economic process are now so complex that they are completely *beyond the capabilities* of any planner or planners to comprehend. But it is to the credit, not the detriment, of the market order that it contains, processes and uses far more information than any single mind could comprehend.

There would be no problem about steering the economy if some central planning board could be sure that it was in possession of all of the necessary information, that it could collect this information fairly cheaply, and that it could make people act on the decisions it made on the strength of the information before it. But in all except the very smallest human groups, the factors to be considered regarding the use of resources is enormous, and it quickly becomes impossible to take a global view of them. As new uses for materials are discovered, or as old sources of supply run out, the facts of economic life constantly change: the information about supply and demand can never be transmitted quickly enough to some central authority, and the personal skill to make use of it cannot be taught to a planning authority. Time would be needed by the planning board to digest what information it had and to disseminate it. By that time, the circumstances of supply and demand will assuredly have changed again.

In other words, the problem of allocating resources in a large economy is a problem of *collecting all the necessary information*, rather than making decisions once we have the data. Therefore:

To assume all the knowledge to be given to a single mind . . . is to assume the problem away and to disregard everything that is important and significant in the real world.[13]

If some authority were able to possess all the relevant information about supply conditions, people's preferences, and the production processes which are available now and in the future, then working out what resources to use where would be just a computational problem. But the millions of individuals in society have their own particular knowledge of local circumstances, which change quickly and which can therefore never be put into the central economic equations. Accidents happen and unforeseen needs arise; even the largest factory cannot definitely predict when it will need new roofing tiles, stationery or any of the other things which must be readily available on the market if it is to function efficiently.[14]

The market order is not something which has been designed and invented by conscious planning: it is the result, the pattern, of many millions of individuals pursuing their own purposes, co-operating with others to the extent that they find it mutually beneficial. This order has not been designed to direct resources; it is the outcome of people's economic activity, the pattern of their individual actions. The general rules which guide their actions, such as the law of property and contract, enable a very complex overall order to emerge; *so* complex that it is *beyond the understanding* of any single mind.[15] To maintain that society must be deliberately planned because it has become complex is therefore paradoxical.

We are all planners: Since Hayek first wrote on the subject, many who are still convinced of the efficacy of planning have reduced its claims in order to suggest how a very complex society could be planned. The most common form this argument takes is that the overall planning of the economy should be undertaken by a central authority, which can look at the problems of the moment and plan out a strategy for tackling them, while the lesser adjustments which are needed to fulfil these strategic plans can continue to be done at the tactical level by businesses.[16]

Yet these arguments for 'balanced growth' or 'indicative planning' are again ill-founded. They ignore the fact that we are all planners in our limited way. Every individual, and every firm, makes guesses about what the future will hold, and how to deal with it. We anticipate changes (correctly or incorrectly) and make sure that we are prepared to make the best of them. An efficient business has this process down to a fine art, although no business or individual (or government, for that matter) could claim perfect foresight. But by anticipating the plans of others, each business or individual reconciles his own purposes with theirs. This skill is the very one which the 'guiding' plan would override: it seems remarkable to suggest that politicians or economists (who as a profession 'have made a mess of things'[17]) could perform it more accurately!

And, moreover, the fact that managers would no longer be adjusting their behaviour to small changes in their immediate environments (i.e. price rises and falls), but would have to understand and accommodate the implications of major national plans and policies, would *reduce* their ability to plan ahead instead of increase it. In this halfway house between planning and the market process, the lives of managers would become critically dependent on the red tape, delay and unpredictability which characterise bureaucratic decisions.

Whatever the magnitude of the economic variables which are taken under the jurisdiction of any plan, planning means *committing ourselves to only one guess* about the future. If it turns out to be accurate, our plans may achieve our purposes, but a wrong guess could bring disastrous consequences. So the more that is covered by any plan, the bigger the guess being made, the greater the possibility of disaster. Where businesses are free to make their own predictions about future demand and supply conditions, only they are at risk. Allowing businesses and individuals to make their own plans, therefore, seems to be infinitely safer than entrusting the guesswork about the future to some central planning board that risks all our futures.

Is it really likely that a National Planning Office would have a better judgement of 'the number of cars, the number of generators, and the quantities of frozen foods we are likely to require in, say, five years,' than Ford or General Motors, etc., and, even more important, would it even be desirable that various companies in an industry all act on the same guess?[18]

The point Hayek wishes to stress here is that the fact that an economic system is not managed centrally does not mean to say that it is 'unplanned'. We all make plans, and businesses succeed if their planning is accurate and efficient, but fail if it is not. The free economy is therefore planned at many centres, instead of just one, and can in consequence make use of the information about local conditions which is available at the individual and company level, but which could not be efficiently communicated to a central authority.

This is not a dispute about whether planning is to be done or not. It is a dispute as to whether planning is to be done centrally, by one authority for the whole economic system, or is to be divided among many individuals.[19]

Planning presupposes a direction: Conscious organisation for a particular purpose is certainly one of the most powerful abilities of the human mind, Hayek reminds us. But like all organisations which are deliberately fashioned, the planned economy must be limited in scope. Conscious direction can certainly achieve a few things very well, like the *Autobahnen* in Germany (and today we would have to add the American moon landing and the impressive armed forces of the Soviet Union). But it cannot co-ordinate all the information needed to run the *whole* of a vast economic system at once; it cannot achieve *all* the objectives which the market order *routinely* satisfies.

The most that we can expect from planning is that it will satisfy, perhaps to a spectacular degree, the ambitions of particular specialists with definite ideas about what ought to be done in their own areas of expertise, be it highway engineering, weapons technology, or science. But it would be difficult to claim that the showpiece achievements of planned economies satisfy much real need: the German Autobahn network was magnificent, but grossly underused. The one thing which the concept of planning does, however, is to unite the idealists and the technical experts who have devoted their lives to a single task, and have a well-formed conception of what society ought to look like. But these very idealists, who are the strongest proponents of planning, would be the most dangerous people to administer it, because they are so intolerant of the competing ideas of others. And hence:

From the saintly and single-minded idealist to the fanatic is often but a step.[20]

The trouble is that we are all 'specialists' in our own aims, and that we all have at least some ideas about what should be done. The command economy cannot co-ordinate all our desires and reconcile them because no planner can comprehend all the information needed. It must choose *a few* purposes and satisfy those to the exclusion of others.

One of the blessings of the free society is that we do not in fact have to agree on common purposes to live and work together, and even to help each other by market exchange. Yet this is seen as a deficiency by planning enthusiasts. Even so, their aims of 'common welfare' or 'social goals' are notable for their lack of content. Even the most determined planners usually fail to agree on the details of what the 'social goals' should be.

While this elegant language might win support for the planning cause, then, it is unlikely to aid the actual plans themselves, because the idea of making plans *presupposes* that they are made for some *particular purpose* and to achieve some particular set of ends. But in society no such agreement exists, and it is doubtful that it could exist in anything but the smallest human groups. Anyone who has wandered the streets for hours in a group looking for a suitable restaurant in a strange city which will be to everyone's liking will recognise the wisdom of Hayek's remark that:

The effect of the people's agreeing that there must be central planning, without agreeing on the ends, will be rather as if a group of people were to commit themselves to take a journey together without agreeing where they want to go; with the result that they may all have to make a journey which most of them do not want at all.[21]

THE DECLINE OF DEMOCRACY

It is this difficulty in deciding what the right aims of the collective economy should be, what benefits should be aimed at first, and how best to achieve them, which starts the socialist state on its journey down the road to serfdom. Hayek pictures the scene: as arguments rage about what purposes should be chosen, parliaments become seen as mere talking shops; even where deliberate targets can be set, there will be further disagreement on how to reach them; and if a route is chosen, the detail of administration required to achieve it will be beyond the scope of an elected body. The conviction will grow in the minds of the public that the social programme should be taken out of the hands of the politicians and entrusted to experts who will be more efficient and less long-winded.

This feeling will gain some measure of support from the politicians themselves, who will feel that they have to delegate a number of administrative decisions because of their technical nature. But this is precisely why these decisions cannot be entrusted to non-elected bodies and officials, for the complexity of the issues that require delegation means that they *cannot be decided by general rules* applying to everyone. The authority is delegated because officials have the time and expertise to decide 'each case on its merits'. This, however, is simply another phrase for the exercise of arbitrary power. Once government agencies have the powers delegated to them to take and enforce decisions at the individual level, the next developments are well known:

. . . once wide coercive powers are given to governmental agencies for particular purposes, such powers cannot be effectively controlled by democratic assemblies.[22]

Even countries where there is only a moderate amount of central control over the economy, like many Western nations, have seen evidence of this development: it is nothing unusual or fanciful. In Britain or the United States, and in many other nominally free societies, there exist government officers, never elected, who have in effect the power to make the law in certain areas; their discretion is wide, and they can favour particular groups if they choose; their whims can be imposed on the general public; and they are not subject to recall by electors. Often there exists no mechanism for challenging their decisions.[23] While these agencies effectively decide the law, their actions can hardly be considered as serving the cause of justice; and Hayek sees this kind of arbitrary and unlimited power as the greatest threat to the free society:

It would scarcely be an exaggeration to say that the greatest danger to liberty today comes from the men who are most needed and most powerful in modern government, namely, the efficient expert administrators exclusively concerned with what they regard as the public good.[24]

Equality before the law: Any society which is determined to push ahead with the socialist ideals of central planning, says Hayek, has to abandon the principles of equal treatment under law. That this cherished ideal must perish cannot logically be avoided.

The first thing which has to collapse is the ancient liberal principle that *government itself must be limited.* The powers of headmen, kings or elected assemblies have always rested on a concensus among their subjects about what those powers should be. There has always been a certain *private sphere* in which government is not entitled to intrude. But if the plans of the central economic authorities are to be successful, nothing must stand in their way; they have to be able to control *all* the economic resources which the nation can muster, or their plans may be thwarted. In other words, the traditional and customary limits to government power must vanish.

There is another sense in which the law must collapse. To achieve their objectives, the planners must direct *particular resources* towards *particular purposes.* The planned economy is not based on the operation of general rules like the market order; it is based on the conscious direction of resources to achieve particular results. As they shift resources from one sector of the economy to another, the planners are constantly having to decide whose views should count most, whose proposals should be accepted, and which workers are available at the time to labour on the accepted plans. And at the individual level, government agencies will have to decide particular cases 'on their merits' and not under a general rule known beforehand and against which people can judge the likely outcome; that is, each decision will be made on the basis of how it is seen to promote the plans in force at that moment, and as such those decisions cannot be anticipated in advance.

It is clear that the law has been abandoned in such circumstances. Where men are placed in employments by the direction of a central authority, they have become mere pieces in a game, subject to whatever arbitrary moves are required to achieve an overall end result. There are no general rules governing what might become of them, no certainties about how the government might dispose of them tomorrow. And again, where the government can foresee how its plans will affect particular people, it cannot be impartial when it makes its choice of objectives. There is no 'blind' justice in such a state; it *must* make choices between individuals.

Hayek's belief is that once the principles of law and the limitation of government powers have been removed in this way, the floodgates are opened to ardent nationalism and the persecution of minorities. This, he says, is a common feature of planned economic systems, and to all those who wish to see how the political consequences of planning appear in practice, he points out that:

... the almost boundless possibilities for a policy of discrimination and oppression provided by such apparently innocuous principles as 'government control of the development of industries' have been amply demonstrated.[25]

Economic freedom means social freedom: It is often suggested that by giving up a measure of *economic* freedom, we can improve our attainment of *other* things we value.

Against this, Hayek observes that economic factors condition our striving for all other ends. When choosing between alternative targets, we evaluate the various things we must give up in order to attain each one, and the benefits which we will enjoy when we do, and we work out the combination of our resources, such as time and money, which will achieve the best results for the minimum outlay. Everything we aim for, then, involves an 'economic' decision; although money may not be the main consideration, we are always evaluating our costs in terms of things we would have to give up to achieve some goal.

Moreover, money is not (except in the perverse case of the miser) an end in itself, but a means to other ends. Money gives people the power to achieve other things they want. A store of wealth gives us the option of doing things in the future which we might not be sure we want to do at the moment, or where we are unsure about what opportunities exist. It is not something we acquire for its own sake. Because the whole of life requires economic calculations, and because economic calculations are necessary to achieve non-economic desires, it is impossible to separate the two cleanly. This means that an authority which has control over the economic process has control over what things people can achieve, and control over what non-economic purposes they will be able to fulfil. It is an awesome power:

Economic control is not merely control of a sector of human life which can be separated from the rest; it is the control of the means for all our ends. And whoever has sole control of the means must also determine which ends are to be served, which values are to be rated higher and which lower, in short, what men should believe and strive for.[26]

The tyranny which this control makes possible is easy to illustrate. In a free society, there are no impenetrable barriers to anyone's ambitions; the problem is only that the same resources are often wanted for many purposes by many people and that it might take a great deal of effort to achieve any particular private goal. But in the planned economy, the barriers are solid; objectives which do not fit in with the approved social goals are simply unobtainable. Hayek gives the examples of the plain girl who badly wants to become a saleswoman and the weak boy who has set his heart on a job where his weakness handicaps him. In the competitive economy, if they value these positions sufficiently, they will quite probably be able to obtain them, albeit at the cost of much initial sacrifice, for their determination and other qualities of character will eventually become obvious. But the planner, in deciding who is fit for which job, would need objective tests; those who were not the standard applicant would fail, and might never be able to achieve their valued ambitions. In the collectivist economy, the individual is merely a means to 'higher' ends and cannot vault the barriers set up by his masters.

These examples show that the alternative to pricing is rationing out opportunities and resources, and even more dire examples could be produced to question the wisdom of having important decisions over an individual's life made by authority and not by the 'economic' valuations of the individual himself. Where medicine is controlled by the state, for instance, the controlling authorities hold the power of life and death over everyone, deciding who should get access to kidney machines, who should receive essential heart surgery, and so on. Hayek believes that it is simply not acceptable that one's peace of mind, health and even life itself should be so decided by authority, but that it is better for individuals to have the opportunity of giving up certain objectives (say, a holiday) to achieve certain others (such as essential surgery).[27]

The conclusion which follows from this is that central planning can never stop at mere economic control, but must spread deeply into the life of a community. Economic control means complete control over everything which people think is worth striving for. So we must be on our guard to protect

... that freedom in economic affairs without which personal and political freedom has never existed in the past.[28]

Economic equality: Once the belief fades that the planned economy can produce the abundance it promised, its theorists and agents have to rely on other ways to justify it. The idea of greater equality before the law is obviously implausible in a society where people are *directed by authority* rather than protected by general rules, and the idea of greater equality of opportunity is hardly appropriate where all opportunities are gifts of the ruling powers. The usual justification for the planned economy at this stage becomes its ability to bring about a 'more equal' spread of wealth or income.

Of course, the problem of sharing resources between everybody is not just an economic problem, but will be the source of much *political* discussion as well:

As soon as the state takes upon itself the task of planning the whole economic life, the problem of the due station of the different individuals and groups must indeed inevitably become the central political problem.[29]

The planners might not wish to redistribute incomes according to any political ideal, but once planning starts, it is difficult to stop income redistribution becoming comprehensive. In particular, when people see themselves as (and politicians reinforce the view that they are) means to some common end, they demand equal reward. Where the hazards of skill and luck and impersonal market forces determine income, inequality may be more easily borne, but in the consciously planned economy, it is harder to accept.

The only simple way to fix rewards in the planned economy, says Hayek, is to have complete equality. But few people think that this is desirable, so the planner usually argues merely for 'fairer rewards' or some other nonspecific phrase which can mean different things to different men. Our concept of what is a 'fair' level of payment for a job come to us because we live in a competitive economy where going wage rates are widely known, although we realise that they will vary over time; but such concepts soon evaporate under socialism. For the planner to decide what is a 'fair wage', he has to make his own arbitrary judgement of the value of individuals or groups, and there are bound to be conflicts when the valuations of the planners disagree with the valuations which people have of themselves.

Thus we see a tug-of-war between various groups, all trying to get a larger share of the income cake from the controlling authorities. And it is by no means certain that the poorest groups would prevail in this struggle. The well-organised groups, the articulate people, the professional lawyers or engineers or teachers on the fringes of government, are likely to have far more political muscle than the unorganised ranks of the very poor.[30]

Undoubtedly this conflict will stimulate severe political differences, which will have to be removed if the planning function is to continue undeterred. At this stage, there might even arise alternative forms of socialism, such as the national socialism in Germany which appealed directly to the very poor over the heads of the mighty trade unions. Hayek himself does not elaborate further, but anyone who has seen the bitter doctrinal disputes among rival brands of socialism will take the point.

WHY THE WORST GET ON TOP

Once the elected assemblies of the socialist state have devolved administrative power upon bodies of non-elected experts, there arises the problem of co-ordinating all government activities and making sure that there are no clashes of purpose. At this stage, says Hayek, the calls for strong leadership (which have always been present, owing to the apparent inability of the elected bodies to agree) become strident, because the planning process now seems to need a leader who is determined enough to make sure that things get done.

If such a leader, or group of leaders, is to arise, it will require strength and a relative absence of scruples. After all, in the planned economy where the creation of wealth (and hence other objectives) is controlled, power is the only thing worth having, and there will be many aspiring candidates. Historically, as in Germany, true socialists shy away at this stage, for they are inhibited by their ideals. But others are not, and many less squeamish souls are attracted by the heightened power which is available in the collectivist economy, harnessing the effort of many millions of individuals, and certainly greater than any power to be found in a free economy.[31]

Once a strong leader arises, it is difficult to stop him. There may be criticism, but his opponents will be divided in their own views about what ought to be done, and will find it hard to combine. Parliament may be retained, and may even prevent some abuses of power. But in order to control the economy and society, the economic leader must have all available resources of power at his disposal, which reduces the effect of any countervailing efforts by others.

To consolidate his position, the strong leader relies on the mass of individuals with uncomplicated attitudes. He will undoubtedly latch on to the grievances which planning has already caused, and he will find allies in the docile and the gullible. A perceived enemy is a useful demagogic device, and it is usual, Hayek insists, for dictatorial socialism (which is what it has become at this stage) to become very nationalistic in its outlook. For collectivism, whatever its claims, is really applied to a limited group or nation; who wants world equality of income, or for the capital resources built up in a collectivist regime to be spread throughout other countries? Socialism may be internationalist in theory, but it is nationalistic and imperialistic in fact. And those are two qualities for which Hayek has on more than one occasion stated his particular contempt.

The moral qualities of collectivism: It becomes easier for a dictator to arise because the moral qualities which are valued in the collectivist society are quite different from those of liberal orders and tend to support the powers of authority. In liberal societies, people are not constrained, or even urged, to do particular things; they are free to act provided that they do so within certain minimal rules of conduct. But the collectivist morality requires the performance of particular duties selected by authority, and the acquisition of 'useful habits' which contribute to the central plan.

Once the individual becomes a means to serve some ultimate end, says Hayek, the most horrific events become possible. The happiness of the individual, for example, becomes an almost useless datum in the calculus of the collectivity. Dissent must be suppressed because it could unnerve people or even deflect them from the approved goals. Individuals must expect to be uprooted and deployed at the direction of authority in order that they serve the social goals most efficiently.

With such cruelty being a moral duty, the totalitarian leader and his executive will have to be individuals who are able to break every kind of moral rule which is appropriate in the liberal society. But totalitarian states have not historically been short of such men.

Suppression of truth: There is one part of this process which Hayek finds so important that he devotes an entire chapter of *The Road to Serdom* to it, and that is the manipulation of information.[32]

The totalitarian economic plan requires that people should believe in the chosen ends, and the traditional way of ensuring this has been the control of current information about alternatives. The moral issue here is not whether the chosen ends are good or bad, but the problem that propaganda steadily undermines the respect for truth. Perversions of the old liberal morality will be required to inspire acceptance of the new; words will have to change their meaning to support this; the planner will have to rationalise his decisions for public consumption, since in reality he has no way to make the necessary choices on known moral principles; the prejudices of the planners will be elevated into 'scientific' theories; and so on. To help stem public criticism of the totalitarian regime, schools have to be used to spread solidarity; information from abroad will be controlled; and eventually the lessons of history, law and economics will have to be re-cast to save the goals which everyone regards as so important. By this time (says Hayek with the sigh of bitter experience) the change in the meaning of words will have imposed barriers on rational discussion of social or economic theory; and indeed the whole of abstract thought, since it is outside the purposes of the state and may prove harmful to them, will be discouraged. But this corruption of truth is not an accidental by-product of collectivism; it is necessary to the survival of fixed collective goals.

It is often argued that people in the competitive economy are similarly manipulated by distorted information, particularly advertising. But in the competitive economy nobody can *prevent* free thought, nor limit it to serve a particular purpose. Indeed, the competitive economy survives on the introduction of new ideas, new methods and new products, and puts a high premium on them. If the collectivist theories and social goals are not to be killed by new ideas and new facts, however, these ideas have to be discouraged and the facts must be changed.

THE IMPACT OF HAYEK'S CRITIQUE OF SOCIALISM

It is clear that *The Road to Serfdom* did much to arrest the utopian social theories of many intellectuals of the time. It was not a work which had been designed to explain the actual development of totalitarianism in Nazi Germany, although it undoubtedly did. Nor was it intended to suggest that such a decline into totalitarianism would be inevitable once we had set foot on the road. But it did certainly show that the unforeseen but inevitable consequences of socialist planning create a state of affairs in which – if the planning policies continue to be pursued – totalitarian forces will get the upper hand.

For this reason, the book was instrumental in helping a number of influential figures understand the consequences of their idealistic proposals. Even Lord Keynes, nowadays the patron saint of a number of socialist economists, could write of it that he found himself 'in agreement with virtually the whole of it; and not only in agreement with it, but in deeply moved agreement'.[33] It certainly did not stop the politicians, or prevent a Labour government committed to massive social and economic reorganisation from being elected in Britain after the war. But that government, while successful in laying the foundations of the welfare state (the inevitable and chronic cracks in their masonry would not be noticed until later), did not reap much success from its programme of industrial nationalisation. In his Foreword to the American edition of 1956, Hayek was able to say that this setback for socialism in Britain had given the liberals a breathing space – but no more than that.[34]

Many of the liberals are still holding their breath. One of the most powerful themes of *The Road to Serfdom* is that even modest economic planning has the effect of slowly but inexorably eroding the values and attitudes which are vital if freedom is to exist. When it is believed that jobs can be created by the government and not by employers serving the customer; when we suppose that incomes can be made secure and unaffected by the constant changes of the market; and when the government starts to protect the monopolies and special privileges of particular groups for whatever reason, then the erosion of liberty has begun. Before long, people see their future lying with government protection and direction, instead of the free and competitive economy.

It is to this well-intentioned but unworkable effort to make jobs and incomes secure from the realities of the market, and to promote 'social justice' by economic engineering, that Hayek addressed a large portion of *Law, Legislation and Liberty* and later writings.

CHAPTER FOUR

The Criticism of Social Justice

To discover the meaning of what is called 'social justice' has been one of my chief preoccupations for more than 10 years. I have failed in this endeavour – or rather, have reached the conclusion that, with reference to a society of free men, the phrase has no meaning whatever.[1]

A MAJOR purpose of *The Road to Serfdom* was to show that economic planning, aimed at the achievement of particular collective targets, necessarily leads to increasing coercion of individuals to a point that no idealistic socialist would ever wish to see. While the 'hot socialism' which Hayek was criticising there 'is probably now a thing of the past',[2] some of its conceptions have penetrated deeply into the minds of men in the West. There has grown up a body of opinions, now much more widespread than that calling for complete economic planning, which believes that the social and economic order can be adjusted in a more modest way to achieve 'social justice'. Many politicians and thinkers, while not advocating economic planning, nevertheless believe that 'social legislation' can be used to promote 'social rights' or 'social awareness' and 'social responsibility'.

Having earlier dealt with the strong collectivist ideologies, Hayek's later works turn to mop up these others. His criticism is constructed on many columns: he finds that such 'social policy' undermines the attitudes which genuinely promote freedom, thwarts the beneficial effects of a free society and free economy, and stems from a misunderstanding of true justice.

WHY 'SOCIAL JUSTICE' HAS NO MEANING

Justice is a different concept, because it is generally used in two different ways. The first indicates what one person is due from another under some general rule.[3] For example, if someone renegues on a business contract for personal gain, or steals property from another, then it is a case of injustice. There are general rules about this kind of activity, and these 'rules of justice' help us to live and co-operate together by allowing us to be reasonably confident about what others will or will not do, although we might still argue about what the rules should be, or whether one should override another (for example, if somebody stole in order to prevent a greater injustice being done in some other way).

The important thing about justice, however, is that it is something which applies to human *conduct*, where individuals are expected to act in a certain way and have a choice in the matter. If a person contracts a disease, or suffers the loss of a relative, or is born with a physical defect, it may be unfortunate, but it is not 'unjust'. It is simply a fact of nature, and has nothing to do with just or unjust action. Justice is a moral concept, and only human beings and their deeds can be called moral or immoral, virtuous or wicked, just or unjust.[4]

The second use of the word 'justice' does not refer to general rules of conduct between people, but to the distribution of things between them. This is 'social justice', sometimes called 'distributive justice', and it is used to imply that a particular distribution of wealth or income or other desirables between the various members of a society (usually a more equal distribution) is fairer and more just.

But Hayek insists that this second sense of justice, this notion of 'social justice', is quite meaningless in a free society. For in the competitive economy, only a mixture of individuals' skill and luck determines where they will be placed on the ladder of income and wealth. Their relative position is not the result of anyone's deliberate action, but the outcome of a process over which nobody has any control. It is therefore mistaken, or fraudulent, to use the word 'injustice' about it or to suggest that another outcome would be more 'just', because nobody has acted unjustly.

There is no doubt that the concept of 'social justice' has captured the public imagination. Hayek observes that it is almost impossible for modern politicians not to appeal to it in support of their various measures. And since this 'just distribution' of income and wealth can be achieved (it is supposed) merely by tax changes, it has become the chief promise of socialist parties, replacing their exaggerated claims of abundance by planning. Yet the near-universal acceptance of a belief does not prove that it is valid, nor does the use of a word mean that there exists anything which it stands for. A universal belief in witches or ghosts does not mean that they exist, for example; in Hayek's view, the phrase 'social justice' is much like the word 'witch', a term which refers to something that does not exist.

'Social justice' and the free society: The reason why 'social justice' has no meaning in the free society can be traced back to Hayek's explanation of society as the undesigned product of an evolutionary development, as an order which has 'grown' without anyone intending it. Because the outcome is unintended, it cannot be discussed in terms of 'justice'.

The social order grows up because individuals act within general rules of universal application. The emergence of a social order is only possible because individuals act in certain fairly predictable ways with respect to one another; and the groups which have the most effective sets of personal rules of conduct will survive and expand more easily than others. But the overall effect of observing the rules cannot be known in advance, just as the winners of a game cannot be deduced from looking at the rules. Society is a complex phenomenon, and the individuals who comprise it are complex themselves; it is impossible to know with any certainty how any individual's actions will be valued by others in the marketplace, nor how they will react to his actions, nor how others in turn will react to them; so the overall outcome is completely unpredictable.

This phenomenon is particularly clear in the economic process, for instance in the development of new products. While everyone might adhere to the rules of the market system, it is impossible to predict which individuals are likely to discover a source of new demand, who else will be able to satisfy that demand, who will consistently outperform his competitors to profit from it, and where changes in demand or supply conditions will force others out of the market. The overall outcome depends on a mixture of skill and luck and the unforeseeable actions of countless other individuals.

It may be that we do not like the outcome: that someone who has worked hard loses heavily, for example, or that an individual who is regarded as an obnoxious character captures the largest share of the market. We may cry out against the 'injustice' of such a state. But our complaints, however strongly felt, are inappropriate in the market order, because the outcome is not due to the intentions or actions of any definable individual or group. We could not answer the question of *who* had been unjust.

Since the operation of the market depends on the adherence to general rules of conduct, guiding how individuals should behave with respect to each other, a breach of one of these rules would certainly be an injustice. But if nobody breaks the rules, nobody has acted unjustly. A sufferer would have no just complaint against anyone else, all of whom have behaved correctly even though some have gained more than others from so doing. And, most important, we must remember the impossibility of deliberately tailoring the rules of just conduct so that they would produce a more equal overall order; the complexity of society and our limited understanding of the function and full effects of the rules we follow conspire against any such effort at re-designing the economic process. There are no conceivable rules of just individual conduct which would at the same time secure a functioning social and market order and would prevent everyone from being disappointed, says Hayek.[5]

Once again the analogy of game-playing can help us understand this point. In a game, we do not try to fix the outcome to match some preconceived idea of what results would be 'just'. We certainly require that the game is *played* fairly, by the rules, without cheating, but it would be a pointless exercise if the losers could insist that the outcome was overturned every time. And how could the players play towards some specific results? There is no consistent strategy which they could adopt which would make the outcome certain in advance, and the more players in the game, the more impossible it would be to ensure the specified outcome.

The presumption of common purposes: The belief in 'social justice' stems, therefore, from a misconception of society. It supposes that society is deliberately organised. Generally, it suggests that 'society' is a sort of person who can allocate the rewards that he gives to us. Society is definitely not such a person, however. It is a complex but unplanned system of values and actions, a pattern of reconciled aims, not shared ones. Many of the benefits we have are indeed due to the operation of this complex structure, but they are *not* the result of anyone's *intention* to bestow benefits on us.

It is because people tend to think of society as an individual whose personality is the sum of the people who comprise him that the adherents of 'social' objectives make another great mistake. This is the error that there is any basis for agreement about what overall outcome is desirable. Part of the appeal of 'social justice' may well be that it leaves undefined exactly what is being aimed at and so it can be all things to all men. As Hayek puts it,

... the word 'social' *presupposes* the existence of known and common aims behind the activities of a community, *but does not define them.* It is simply assumed that 'society' has certain concrete tasks that are known to all and are acknowledged by all, and that 'society' should direct the endeavours of its individual members to the accomplishment of these tasks.[6]

But 'society' is not such a single individual with a single purpose, and no agreement exists on what common aims should be adopted. The adoption of common aims (an impossible ideal in any case) would require a complete abandonment of our present morality, since only the outcomes, and not the fixed and general rules guiding behaviour between individuals, would be important.

This last point is of the utmost significance. The values that make our civilisation possible are values which promote our adherence to general rules of conduct. The outcome of our behaviour within those rules is useful and beneficial, but unplanned by any individual or group. If 'social justice' is to be accepted as a new moral value, it requires human behaviour to be aimed at a particular *purpose*, not simply *restrained* by general rules. Our traditional values, our existing morality, would have to be sacrificed.[7] In the same way that we cannot make the rules of a game determine a particular outcome, there is no way in which we can combine any general rules of economic behaviour with a predetermined distribution of income or wealth. As Hayek concludes on the matter:

There exists no third principle for the organisation of the economics process which can be rationally chosen to achieve any desirable ends, in addition to either a functioning market in which nobody can conclusively determine how well-off particular groups or individuals will be, or a central direction where a group organised for power determines it.[8]

UNDERMINING THE ATTITUDES OF FREEDOM

Hayek believes, then, that the endorsement of some moral principle based on 'social' outcomes must undermine the subtle morality of the rules upon which present civilisation is founded, rules whose functions we can scarcely understand. There are many different ways in which the attitudes conducive to freedom begin to evaporate when 'social justice' becomes the aim.

'Value to society': Hardly any adherent of the belief in 'social justice' would argue that there should be complete equality of incomes. For that would guarantee equal rewards to everyone, no matter how lazy or even deliberately obstructive he chose to be. And there seems on the surface to be a much stronger case for rewarding people in relation to the amount of effort or merit they display in their work. It is therefore most commonly argued that 'social legislation' should be seeking to achieve a distribution of rewards on the basis not of complete equality but of each person's 'value to society'.

To Hayek, this phrase 'value to society' is another carelessly used term which turns out to be meaningless. It suggests once again that 'society' is some sort of person who benefits from what we contribute to him. But in reality a service can have value only to a real person, and different members of a society might well value the same service very differently. The social order has no agreed aims, is not designed to achieve any particular targets, and is based not on a hierarchy of values but on the different and often conflicting values of its various members. It is therefore a mistake to suggest that some individuals or their services can be more or less 'valuable' to something which has no values of its own.

The point can be illustrated with various examples. Even the performance of a Beethoven sonata, a painting by Leonardo or a play by Shakespeare have no 'value to society', says Hayek, but only to those who know and appreciate them. A boxer, a singer and a violin virtuoso render services to different groups of different numbers of people; but it would be impossible to say which contributed the greatest 'value to society' because the enjoyment of these different groups simply cannot be measured against each other.

How then can we possibly decide the appropriate remuneration for particular services? It is certainly true that the relative incomes prevailing in different professions may not always agree with people's opinions of what they deserve, and many object to the 'injustice' of such a state of affairs, saying that money incomes do not reflect the 'value to society' of the various groups. But, Hayek counters:

. . . when we ask what ought to be the relative remunerations of a nurse and a butcher, of a coal miner and a judge at a high court, of the deep sea diver of the cleaner of sewers, of the organizer of a new industry and a jockey, of the inspector of taxes and the inventor of a life-saving drug, of the jet pilot or the professor of mathematics, the appeal to 'social justice' does not give us the slightest help in deciding. . .[9]

The rewards of the market: The prizes which the market process offers are a much surer guide of how much the services of one individual are worth to his fellows than any arbitrary standard of 'value to society'. The prices paid to the provider of a service will not normally depend on the judgement of any one person, but upon the number of others providing the service, the number demanding it, and the urgency of the need which the buyers feel. Each service in a free society, then, is rewarded according to the very personal or subjective value placed upon it by many different individuals who benefit from it.

It is not surprising, therefore, that the rewards of the market may not correspond to any notion of 'just compensation' (in the sense that someone is rewarded according to an objective measure of the time and energy or skill that he puts into some job). The level of those rewards will depend upon complex values and relationships between many suppliers and many buyers, and will be merely the outcome of a process of exchange in which they all take part because they all benefit. It will be an outcome that is neither right nor wrong, just nor unjust, simply a fact; but it will reflect in some measure the value which particular services have to the individuals who make up the functioning market order.

Reward and merit: A person's reward in the market is *not* a function of the personal effort he makes and the degree of pain and suffering he undergoes to produce the service, nor of his moral merits. Often, people find a value in others because of some natural ability they have, rather than any great effort they are prepared to make. A fine voice or a ready wit are marketable capacities, and worth something to others, even though the people exhibiting these capacities need not make any great personal sacrifice in the process of marketing them, and may indeed be reprehensible characters.

It would be a mistake, then, to suppose that people should be rewarded on the basis of some standard of personal worth or merit – another suggestion often made by the advocates of 'social justice'. What a man's services are worth to others bears no relation to how much effort he is prepared to invest; indeed, some people enjoy their job so much that they might even do it for nothing. Nor does the worth of a service to others depend upon the good or bad personal qualities of the supplier. It is as much a commendation of competition as of justice that it is no respecter of persons.[10] Nor does a supplier's worth to others depend upon whether his product is the outcome of years of investment and effort, or whether he was only lucky. Indeed, there is probably no way to calculate how much of any supplier's trade is due to his skill and how much to luck. Thus, Hayek concludes, it is neither practicable nor desirable in a free society to ask that rewards should correspond to what people normally recognise as merit.[11]

If we are to allocate rewards on the basis of merit, we also have the severe problem of *assessing* that merit. But to measure someone's merit is impossible: it is a subjective thing. Diligent effort may lead to failure, success may come through accident, so outcomes alone would not be sufficient. Any panel of judges would face an immense task in trying to work out whether the failures should be compensated because of the merit that went into them, or whether the successes should be penalised because they were lucky.

Indeed, there is an important sense in which we *want* services to be provided with the *minimum* of merit on the part of the supplier – the sense in which everyone gains where a service is provided as cheaply as possible. We want to *reduce* the amount of pain and sacrifice which goes into the production of any commodity, particularly where that effort or those sacrifices could have been used more productively elsewhere. Any attempt to reward people for their actual sacrifices would simply encourage personal sacrifice, not induce people to benefit others. No economic order could function on such a principle.[12]

These points all serve to show that the idea of justice is plainly inappropriate when discussing the rewards of the market process. To suggest that the impersonal system of the market order can be just or unjust is rather like saying that a stone can be moral or immoral.[13] The use of the term 'social justice', therefore, rests on a totally mistaken view of what true justice is all about.

Redistribution and equal treatment: There is another important way in which Hayek perceives the idea of 'social justice' as contributing to an erosion of the attitudes and morality which underpin a free society. Redistribution, clearly, requires that people should not be treated equally, and so shatters the principle of the equal application of rules of conduct. Since people differ in many attributes that are difficult or impossible to alter, such as strength, intelligence, skill, resourcefulness and perseverance, as well as in their social circumstances and

94

physical surroundings, a government would have to treat them very differently to compensate for all those advantages and disadvantages.

But there is a more profound reason why the attempt to equalise incomes requires unequal treatment. This is that under such a system, the guiding force of the competitive economy breaks down. In the market, prices guide people into appropriate courses of action; high prices for a particular product prompt people to turn their resources to work to supply it, and low prices discourage the concentration of productive resources on the less remunerative articles. Supply is thereby boosted or diminished to meet the market demand. But if rewards do not reflect market needs, then the system loses its automatic pilot. If a government insists on equality of rewards, therefore, it can only ensure that goods are produced by forcing people into particular occupations as and when it thinks these are needed. Each person must be assigned a task wholly on the grounds of efficiency or what is needed *at the time*, instead of according to any known and uniform rules. This is a very great step away from the concept of a liberal government which is itself constrained by general rules.

Power politics: Once a government takes upon itself the task of redistributing incomes on the basis of some measure of merit or 'social justice' (which must itself be arbitrary), then it will be faced with many competing demands by different individuals and groups. All will claim that their efforts are more meritorious than others, and that their share should be increased. Because there are no agreed rules which help to decide who should get what, the decisions of the government will be arbitrary and unpredictable. Because the initial objectives of income redistribution are unclear, the government will invent confused rules, perhaps satisfying sectional demands, but also preventing the market system from functioning. The lack of any clear and general rules for government action leads to a disrespect for general rules in the minds of the members of society, and so we find that:

Once politics becomes a tug-of-war for shares in the income pie, decent government is impossible.[14]

One of the principal sectional interests calling for a greater share of income will probably be the industries where changing market conditions are leading to a smaller demand for their products. In the market, this would simply be adjusted to; resources would be moved away from those industries, jobs in them would be lost, but people would find employment elsewhere. But when 'social justice is the guiding force, the government will face pressure to protect the falling incomes of people in these industries, or to grant them special privileges. This will, of course, smother the signalling function of prices, and will ensure that more resources are concentrated in such industries than demand requires. The special treatment given to this group will also inspire counter claims from others; and every intervention into the determination of prices and incomes will simply increase the misallocation and require further intervention to solve.

Incomes, therefore, will come to be decided not on the worth which a supplier or an industry has to its customers, but on the ability of different groups to persuade the government of the merits of their case. This in turn may not rest on anything which would be viewed by anyone as genuine merit, but upon the *political influence* of the group in question, and the political damage which could be done to the government if they are not appeased. Accordingly it seems clear that:

... a parliament or government which becomes a charitable institution thereby becomes exposed to irresistible blackmail. And it soon ceases to be the 'deserts' but becomes exclusively the 'political necessity' which determines which groups are to be favoured at general expense.[15]

While the appeal to 'social justice' is commonly directed to the 'social responsibility' of individuals, it is clear that it extinguishes true responsibility. The government, and not the individual, becomes responsible for a person's position in society; but the individual is also urged to be 'socially responsible', a phrase without any clear meaning whatever. The notion of personal responsibility therefore becomes inverted and confused.[16]

Nationalism: There is one last way in which 'social justice' tends to erode the moral foundations of freedom, and that is its tendency to exclude outsiders. Common agreement about the proper material rewards or status of individuals is unlikely to occur except in small communities where people are roughly aware of the relative importance of each other's contributions. Demands for 'social justice', therefore, rarely extend beyond the frontiers of a nation, except possibly in utopian theory.

Hayek perceives a marked tendency, therefore, towards nationalism in those countries where 'social justice' is attempted. When other countries are added to the equation, it becomes evident that there is no possible international standard of 'social justice'. Furthermore, those groups which are in the vanguard of appeals for 'social justice' and for the raising of their own wages are in practice the first to reject similar claims on behalf of foreigners.[17] This kind of nationalism Hayek finds particularly distasteful.

WHY INCOME REDISTRIBUTION STRANGLES GROWTH

The effect of the unhampered processes of the market will be that many people will end up with more than their fellows think they deserve, and others will end up with less. The problem besetting any attempt at redistribution, however, is that incomes are the result of a dynamic market process, a process which slows down and becomes inefficient when any such attempt is made, with the result that there quickly becomes less to share out. It simply is not true that there is an income 'pie' which can be redistributed, and that the process of producing the pie can then continue unabated until the next redistribution. The product of the market process is dynamic, growing all the time, and any attempt to redistribute it at any point thwarts its future growth. The object of policy in a free society, according to Hayek, should not be to redistribute incomes on some rather arbitrary notion of 'social justice', therefore, but to help the total product to grow as large and as rapidly as possible, so that the size of the share of any individual, taken at random, is maximised.

The role of the rich: The divergence in incomes has a significant influence on the growth of the total product over time, and the high gains of the successful individuals, whether arising from effort or accident, are an essential element for guiding resources to where they will make the greatest contribution to future incomes. The inequality which so many people resent is, in fact, the magnetic force which draws up the level of all incomes, and enables people in the West to enjoy the relatively high incomes which most of them do today. And we are on an escalator we cannot step off; the increasing population of the world, a population which is supported by the market system, requires the output of the market to grow. Were it to be sacrificed to some notional idea of equality, it would be the very poorest citizens of the globe who would suffer the greatest hardship.

In addition to their example to others who seek to attain their incomes and thereby contribute to the further satisfaction of market demand, the richer people have another important role from which we all benefit. This is the essential testing of new products which goes on all the time in the free society. At any time, the state of technology is such that there will be many things we can produce, but only at high cost. We do not know which of these possibilities will prove to satisfy human demands until they have been tried in the marketplace.

Richer people therefore play an important role in testing the products which are so expensive that they are luxuries today, but may be commonplace objects tomorrow when they have proved their worth and can be produced in larger numbers. The rich are able to afford new products, and their preferences for some over others draw resources into the production of the more successful ones. The elimination of the less successful products releases resources to be used in more productive ways. As the field of possibilities narrows, and the number of alternative products is reduced to the better ones, the search for new production methods and the development of new refinements becomes more concentrated, and the successful products become available at less cost. This stimulates demand from less wealthy people who can now afford the new product; and so on, until eventually the production cost of the commodity puts it within the grasp of nearly everyone.

Hayek maintains that if people today are able to enjoy having a car, a radio or a refrigerator, or to take an air trip at modest cost, it is because only a few years ago these things were put on the market as undreamed-of luxuries for all but a few.[18] Many of the improvements we take for granted would never have been possible without this process of experimentation, refinement and cheaper production.

We need the rich, therefore, because the market process is dynamic, always developing. So necessary is this service of experimentation, and so useful is it to the rapid expansion of the horizons of the poorer members of society, that Hayek believes it to be essential in any society. Even in a centralised economy, there would have to be a class of people whose lifestyles and whose experience could be passed on to the rest. In the command economy, of course, they would probably be chosen by the authorities, a process which seems far less fair than having them chosen dispassionately and impersonally by the market. But only a society which contained some such class of experimenting persons could hope to keep improving its knowledge about what future options were possible, and could hope therefore to improve rapidly the conditions of even its poorest members.

There is another set of arguments to support the usefulness of the role played by wealthy individuals.[19] In having the resources to back their beliefs, wealthy people can take risks, pushing forward the frontiers of possible production even further, and of course generating employment in the process. Secondly, they can back their beliefs even where there is no prospect of a material return, such as in the sponsorship of the arts, education, research, and the propagation of new ideas in politics, morality and so forth. The wealthy man, seizing upon a deserving cause, can often rally far more resources to it, both from his own efforts and from those who follow him, than any patronage dispensed by political institutions. Thirdly, a class of wealthy individuals may be able to resist some of the more oppressive measures of an unrestrained government.

Though the lifestyle of many wealthy men may seem absurdly lavish, it is a relative matter; the lifestyle of an ordinary American below the national average probably seems absurdly lavish and wasteful to many in China or Africa. In any case, even such an advanced lifestyle will produce experiments and innovations which will gradually percolate through to the other sectors of society, developments which might not otherwise have been possible.

The resentment of the poor: We must remember that the economy is dynamic, and that individuals who are poor today (in addition to the benefits they enjoy because of the role of the rich in prompting new development) may be drawn into developing industries by high wage rates and therefore not remain poor for long. But Hayek considers the case of those who are in jobs which may be dangerous or dirty, but which are not well paid, as is commonly the case. Does justice not demand a greater reward?

Once again, we must remember that society is not a person who organises people into different occupations. If a boss or person in authority placed people of equal capacities in different jobs, some clean and pleasant, others hard, dirty and dangerous, then we should undoubtedly be justified in calling for some compensation to those in the hard, dangerous or dirty jobs, and right to say that an injustice had been done. But the situation is entirely different when we are talking about free men who sell their services to whoever pays them most. People whose aptitudes, and therefore remunerations, may be smaller for more pleasant occupations will often find that they can in fact earn more by taking a less pleasant job. Indeed, the fact that these jobs will be avoided by those who have aptitudes for better ones will help to bid up the wage rates prevailing in them. Market forces therefore do not mean that dirty and unpleasant jobs are always low paid; the market pays well for services which are urgently needed but reluctantly provided.

So all the arguments of justice and merit still apply here. The position of someone in an unpleasant job could only be regarded as unjust if somebody had assigned him that job unjustly. But his position is in fact the outcome of his own desires or seizing of opportunities, and of impersonal market forces. And, once again, who is to assess what the 'value to society' of any such job is? The only meaningful standard is what that job is worth to those who purchase the service.

Inheritance: There is another thing which is often the target for 'social policy', and that is inheritence. The argument takes two forms: the first is based on the belief that everyone should have an equal starting position at birth, without background advantages of family and upbringing; and the second is that parents' wealth should not be passed on to their children, although other, uncontrollable advantages might be.

The equal starting position is clearly impossible to achieve. If we let children remain with their parents, it would mean redistributing all the wealth of parents 'fairly', and keeping it that way while the children grow up. The problem of controlling all the physical and human environments of all persons would be an insuperable one. It would be no less difficult if children were taken from their families at birth and raised in 'equal environments', because still the special advantages of location, the skill of the people raising the children, and so on, would generate important differences, differences which would widen as the children grew up. Attractive as the idea of equality of opportunity may be, it is a wholly illusory ideal, complains Hayek, which would produce a nightmare world if it were attempted.[20]

The less utopian view that children should not enjoy the wealth which parents would like to leave to them is no less problematic. Hayek takes as read the arguments that passing on wealth is essential in avoiding the dispersal of capital and acts as a spur to its accumulation by others.[21] And he does not mention the obvious point that it seems unjust for a government to turn a child out of his home simply because his parents die, even if their wealth is to be generally distributed.

Hayek points out that there are many parts to a person's upbringing besides money, and that it is normally accepted that the family is the best institution to look after them. Parents are more likely than any teacher to make sure their children are given a grasp of the cultural values which are essential to life in society. Secondly, people enjoy and benefit from the qualities of others, even though they result from pure chance, like a good voice or wit; it is difficult to see why the same kind of useful qualities should not be equally valuable when they are the product of a good home or intelligent parents. Thirdly, there are many cultural qualities which are rarely achieved in a single generation, but a family may achieve them over the course of two or three.[22]

Once we recognise that it is desirable to harness the natural instincts of parents to equip the new generation as well as they can culturally, which benefits the whole community, it is difficult to see why the same principle should not apply to material benefits as well. Of all the ways which parents have of helping their children, leaving them money is probably the cheapest socially. Without this outlet, parents tend to provide for their children by getting them into jobs by nepotism, so that whether they are qualified or not they are still guaranteed an income. This is a common phenomenon in communist societies, but it is clear that the practice is inefficient and undesirable.

But the main objection to all of these egalitarian suggestions must be that they require increased and arbitrary government interference to try to redress the imbalances which exist. This in turn requires that governments should treat people unequally, which is a certain way of inducing disrespect for the known and general rules of morality and personal behaviour upon which civilisation is founded.

SOURCES OF THE 'SOCIAL JUSTICE' IDEA

Hayek investigates the origin of the concept of 'social justice' and suggests some disturbing sources.

One of the main complaints against the whole market order is that the changing circumstances of the market leave some people worse off than they used to be. As supply and demand change, it is entirely natural that some individuals and industries will prosper and others will find times harder and harder. This has an essential signalling function, indicating that men should move from the less profitable industries to the more profitable ones, and divert their resources to where their services are more urgently needed.

The groups who are badly hit may be very loud and persuasive in their demands for 'social justice', because the harm that they suffer is concentrated upon them, while the benefits which would accrue to all if they cut their losses and moved to new industries are less obvious. Everyone can see the ills caused by falling wages and unemployment; but nobody can perceive the diffused benefits which this normal part of market adjustment will bring. Politically, therefore, such groups tend to have a great deal of power; but that is not to say that their cause is 'just':

The chief insight we must hold on to is that not always when a group of people have strong views about what they regard as their claims in justice does this mean that there exists (or can be found) a corresponding rule which, if universally applied, would produce a viable order. It is a delusion to believe that whenever a question is represented as one of justice it must be possible to discover a rule capable of universal application which will decide the question.[23]

The second source of the notion of 'social justice' is undoubtedly pure envy.[24] This motive may be camouflaged, and perhaps many social reformers do not even recognise it in themselves, but discontent because some people earn more than others certainly inspires much protest. However, it is not the function of the market necessarily to reward all expectations; any system in which people were rewarded according to what they thought they were worth would quickly fail.

A third possibility is the rise of salaried workers who do not understand the workings of the market. When most people worked on the land, as individuals or in small merchanting groups, it was very natural that an understanding of the market process would be quickly learnt and passed on to the next generation. But the emergence of large businesses employing sizeable workforces which are insulated from the everyday workings of the market has begun to erode this. As Hayek puts it,

an ever increasing part of the population of the Western world grows up as members of large organizations and thus as strangers to those rules of the market which have made the great open society possible. To them the market economy is largely incomprehensible.[25]

103

The atavism of social justice: The most important reason why this belief in 'social justice' is so common, however, is that it appeals to deeply seated natural instincts which were appropriate in the small tribal group of hunter-gatherer peoples from which the large modern society gradually emerged. Man may have existed for 10,000 years in sizeable communities based on agriculture and then on industry; but before that he spent at least a hundred times as long in small hunting groups. The size of such a band makes it possible for each member to know the others personally, and for common aims to be agreed; shares can be assigned on agreed standards of merit; and individuals can be given different roles in order to achieve common purposes.

Despite the fact that we have now moved from the small band to the large society of today, most of whose members we do not know and which must therefore be regulated by impersonal rules, our instincts have not been entirely overcome. In fact:

Our instincts tell us, first, that our duty is to serve the visible needs of our known friends; and, second, that the activity that gives us most satisfaction is to join in a common effort for common needs.[26]

For Hayek, the repeated calls for 'social justice' are largely a yearning to return to this comfortable instinctive world, when in fact it was the abandonment of this old morality which made the extended society based on market processes possible. It seems that:

Socialists have the support of inherited instincts, while maintenance of the new wealth . . . requires an acquired discipline.[27]

CONCLUSIONS

Appeals to 'social justice' are certainly not consonant with the acquired discipline upon which the wealth of society is built, according to Hayek. His examination of the origins of the 'social justice' idea leads him to a scathing rejection of it as a sound principle for human action. At worst, he says, it is a dishonest suggestion (and at best a misguided plea) that other people ought to agree to the demands of a special interest group who can give no logical reason why they should be specially treated. 'Social justice' is by no means the innocent expression of goodwill towards the less fortunate that it is commonly supposed to be, but a demand by particular groups for a privileged position. Perhaps worse, it is in Hayek's view the opposite of genuine justice, which is guided by accepted and general rules and is impartial between different individuals and groups.

The appeals for 'social justice' undoubtedly have the backing of strong instinctive emotions to support them; but the emotions on which they are based are appropriate to the tribal hunting group, and not to the modern society which works on entirely different principles of equal treatment and free co-operation. For all these reasons, Hayek believes it is necessary for us to be very cautious whenever the phrase 'social justice' is mentioned; and for his part, he proclaims his opposition to such an intellectually unrespectable idea by saying that:

... I have come to feel strongly that the greatest service I can still render to my fellow men would be that I could make the speakers and writers among them thoroughly ashamed ever again to employ the term 'social justice'.[28]

CHAPTER FIVE

The Institutions of a Liberal Order

> The attitude of the liberal towards society is like that of
> the gardener who tends a plant and in order to create
> the conditions most favourable to its growth must
> know as much as possible about its structure and the
> way it functions.[1]

CREATING THE CONDITIONS FOR A LIBERAL ORDER

ACCORDING to Hayek, the proper role of government is not to
create any particular social order. No government can attempt
to organise society in a certain way, because society is a very
complex phenomenon and is impossible to manipulate
deliberately. The social and market order have grown in
complexity far beyond that which can be understood by any
mind or any proposed planning agency. Consequently:

Liberalism for this reason restricts deliberate control of the overall
order of society to the enforcement of such general rules as are
necessary for the formation of a spontaneous order, the details of
which we cannot foresee.[2]

Letting society flourish requires us to create suitable conditions
for it. The character of the social order is rather like many other
orders which exist in nature, orders which we cannot build
ourselves but which we can allow to grow by creating the right
conditions. We can never produce a complex crystal, for
example, by putting atoms together one by one; but it is easy to
create the conditions in which the atoms will arrange
themselves in such a way.

If we tried to shape our own society by squeezing it to
conform to a hierarchy of values, and to achieve predetermined
ends, we would surely fail. The most we can do is encourage the
formation of a useful overall order by making sure that the rules
of conduct on which it is based are preserved.[3] Hayek believes

that this judicial role of government has become overshadowed by governments taking more and more organisational power upon themselves, and extending the parts of human life which are subject to deliberate manipulation and control. It is a development which he offers an analysis of and an escape from in *Law, Legislation and Liberty.*

For the individual, the difference between a deliberate, planned organisation and the undesigned, free society is that the rules in an organised society *require the performance* of particular tasks. Individuals are assigned particular roles, with different duties, by the command of the authorities. In the free society, however, men are not commanded, or treated unequally; there are only general rules of equal application within which they are free to act and strive for their own purposes. The government of a free society does not issue commands, but ensures the observance of general rules.

Security: Part of this protection of the ordering forces of the free society will of course be their protection from outside enemies (or possibly internal insurrection). For Hayek, the government clearly has an essential role in defence, which requires it to have certain coercive powers, both in the raising of funds to pay for defence, and even in the recruitment of an army in times of emergency. However, provided that the government itself is bound by general rules in these respects, Hayek does not see any major cause for alarm.

Policing is another function which the government will have to ensure is done if the free society is to endure. Making sure that the general rules of conduct are observed may again require some coercive powers by government, not just in the form of punishment, but also in the raising of funds to pay for policing.

And there are other dangers which can extinguish the social order, and whose effects can be minimised only be deliberate organisation of people: dangers such as storms, floods, earthquakes, epidemics and other natural disasters. The prevention of some disasters (such as fires and epidemics) or the rebuilding of social and market relations after them may well require a government which does not only have

107

compulsory powers to organise co-ordinated action, but has the resources at its disposal to overcome the problem. Hayek therefore concludes that:

The task of government is to create a framework within which individuals and groups can successfully pursue their respective aims, and sometimes to use its coercive powers of raising revenue to provide services which for one reason or another the market cannot supply.[4]

Other non-market services: The market system rests on the principle that the provider of a service will be able to charge the people who enjoy that service. There are, of course, many products and services where this would be difficult because it would be hard to provide the commodity to one person without also providing it to others. Defence, policing and the prevention of epidemics largely come into this bracket; so too, says Hayek, do many kinds of information such as land registers, statistics, the certification of quality of some goods, certain roads and civic amenities where it is difficult to charge those (and only those) who use them.

These services will therefore need an element of compulsion if they are to be provided, because many people might recognise the value of the service but would not contribute to its provision if they thought they could enjoy it for nothing.

Government provision is not without its problems for the political theorist, of course, because it appears at first sight that we are commanding everyone to contribute to the supply of certain goods, even though the goods in question may not be wanted by all or even a considerable majority. But Hayek says that it is in fact in the interest of individuals to agree to compulsory levies to provide unmarketable benefits, knowing that even if they do not care for a particular one, there will be other benefits which they want but which other people do not. And it should be remembered that this method of provision is a *second-best* alternative: it is being resorted to only because the more efficient and preferable mechanism of the market cannot be made to work in these areas.

It should also be remembered that the government need not have a monopoly on the provision of these services. Although they may be financed by government through compulsion, they do not need to be administered and provided by government, and, in fact, competitive enterprises may do the job much better. Government should also step down from its coercive role when new developments make pricing possible where it was not before; where wireless transmissions can be received by anyone, for example, pricing is impossible, but if it is available only to those who rent or buy special equipment, the market can begin to operate.[5] And it should also be remembered that many services which are needed but unprofitable are already provided by charitable and voluntary organisations. No government agency, for example, ever devised a scheme so effective as Alcoholics Anonymous or could parallel the work of numerous local groups of people committed to worthwhile community projects.

TAXATION AND THE SIZE OF GOVERNMENT SERVICES

For Hayek, the size of the government sector of the economy is not the test of its legitimacy. That rests exclusively upon whether its use of coercion is limited by rules and whether the rules which it enforces are of equal application and promote the smooth functioning of the social order.

The correct procedure for deciding the size of the public sector, suggests Hayek, is to come to a decision about the size of the tax burden which people will share, and *only then* to decide how it should be spent. The public sector ought to be interpreted as each person agreeing to pay into a common pool from which he draws some services and other people draw others; not everybody paying for all services, whether they use them or not. Thus the decision about the size of the pool can be separated from argument about what services it is 'socially just' to provide for others, and becomes one about the benefits which any individual, picked at random, will derive in return for the contribution he makes.

The history of public finance, of course, has not been such a high-minded affair; generally it has been an attempt to coerce as much from taxpayers, with as little complaint, as possible. The idea that we all contribute according to a general rule, to a common pool of services from which we all draw a particular assortment, has been replaced by the notion of public services as an instrument of 'social justice' and the imposition of heavier taxes on minorities. The belief that any new expenditure will be paid for by others has encouraged the majority to agree readily to new items, requiring subsequent efforts to raise the necessary finance. The result is not that services are tailored to what people can afford, but that means have to be found to finance a public sector which grows by consent but without any regard to costs. Political pressure and the compulsion of others is seen as a cheap way of paying for the services one most desires. Taxes are raised in new ways upon groups that are almost unable to complain.

The principles of taxation: It was with some reluctance that Hayek criticised the notion of a progressive income tax.[6] For the idea of promoting 'social justice' through income redistribution by taxation is so widespread that it is almost impossible to object to it without inviting a bitter response. Yet, as we have seen, the concept of 'social justice' is meaningless in a free society, and is founded on less than laudible motives. A progressive income tax, as an instrument of income redistribution, fails all the same tests.

Hayek agrees that some progression in taxation might be necessary to offset the proportionately heavier burden which indirect taxes put on smaller incomes. But the principle of progression, which has only been effected since the beginning of this century, has come to be used not for this purpose, but as a political and redistributive weapon.

A second argument that is often used to support graduated income taxes is that 'equal sacrifice' means higher taxes on those who have a larger 'ability to pay'. Yet Hayek protests that this is based on woolly thinking. In the first place, it is impossible to compare the 'sacrifice' which different people make when they give up part of their income (or anything else) because it is a purely subjective concept, and impossible to measure between different people. Secondly, as a person's income grows, it requires a larger addition to his wages to spur him to the same amount of extra effort. This might be an argument for a regressive tax, but not for a progressive one. It is clear that this kind of value analysis is inappropriate to the question of income taxation.

Another point about the progressive tax system is that it contributes comparatively little. Only a very small amount of the gross tax revenue comes from the high rates of tax on the largest incomes, so these taxes presumably serve more to gratify the envy of the poorer individuals than to provide material benefits for them. This is closely associated with the point that a progressive system allows the majority to dictate to the minority, and to use the tax system for their own purposes. It has often been not the poorest people, but the articulate and politically organised working and middle classes which have gained most from redistribution, a fact which reinforces this point. Once we have abandoned the rule that people should contribute equally, then we have lost the brakes on the tax system, and opened up the possibility of complete or almost complete expropriation of the higher incomes.

The economic effects of taxation in a dynamic economic system should not be underestimated. Hayek believes that high incomes are essential if new products and processes, expensive at first, are to be tested and later made available to others lower in the income scale. But not only is innovation and experimentation slowed by high marginal tax rates; the signalling function of profits is corrupted. For example, the reward which an individual enjoys for providing a particular service will depend on when he provides it and what his income is at the time. This is not merely a source of injustice but leads to a change and misdirection of resources.

Other economic effects concern savings and investment. As income is taxed away instead of being saved, there is less to be spent on productive investments which will generate wealth and employment in the future; because people cannot enjoy the rewards of any capital which they are able to save, they will use it less productively or even take it abroad; and the inability of people to build up capital means that they cannot challenge existing firms with established capital bases and a dominant share of a market, and so competition is effectively reduced, simply because of the tax.

Having reviewed all these disadvantages of progressive taxes, Hayek suggests that the only reasonable system of taxation would have the majority who decide its level bearing it

111

at the maximum rate, for only then could the expropriation of minorities by majorities be avoided. He believes that attempting to get round the problem by setting an upper limit on a progressive system is itself quite arbitrary and difficult to justify; and it would be too easily altered when the majority decided that extra revenue was required. He suggests that perhaps the simplest general rule would be to fix the maximum admissible marginal tax rate at that percentage of the total national income which the government takes in taxation. This would mean that if the government takes, say, 25 per cent of the national income, then 25 per cent would also be the maximum admissible marginal tax rate.

THE ECONOMIC FRAMEWORK

Hayek believes that in addition to providing certain services which require taxation, government has a duty to avoid concentrations of coercive power, and otherwise to ensure that trade between individuals is as smooth and fair as possible. He has therefore devoted much energy to considering the coercive powers of monopolies of labour and capital, and to the government's role in enforcing standards of economic behaviour.

Critique of trade union powers: Hayek notices a marked discrepancy between the stated objectives of trade unions and their actual performance. They have moved from the laudible aim of 'freedom of association' to become vehicles for the coercion of some workers by others.[7]

Hayek considers remarkably unjust the Trade Disputes Act of 1906, which exempted British unions and their officers from liability for all kinds of wrongs, and the Sherman and Norris-LaGuardia Acts in the United States, which helped to establish practically complete immunity of unions from tort actions. Whatever powers this may have given unions over employers, it has given them far more power over other workers.

The closed shop is a classic example. Here it is argued that all members of a workforce must be union members if the gains won from union pay negotiations are not to be unfairly

112

distributed to 'free riders'. But, counters Hayek, unions cannot raise wages above the level which would obtain in any case in a market order – except, of course, by limiting supply. So either the 'free riders' are getting the market rate in any case, or the higher rates have been won in return for other workers being squeezed out of jobs or not being employed at all. Unions may benefit their members for a short time; but they do not raise wages above the free market level for all workers in the long term. Indeed, the only reason why a trade union is able to improve the wages of its own members in a closed shop is because it has the coercive power to prevent the employment of outsiders – otherwise the threatened employer could immediately hire non-union labour at the market rate. As Hayek says:

It can hardly be denied that raising wages by the use of coercion is today the main aim of unions.[8]

The net effect of this coercion, however, is to keep workers who are worse off from improving their position, relegating larger numbers to the lower-paid jobs or to the unemployment rolls. This creates a greater *inequality* of wages than would prevail in the free market, and probably depresses the average. It certainly reduces the productivity of labour, since its allocation is determined not by market returns, but by coercion.

A large economy, says Hayek, can remain prosperous only if it relies on competitive forces to co-ordinate individual effort and to steer resources where they are most needed. But when wages are determined by coercion and not by competitive forces, then the overall prosperity of society must suffer. Hence, the belief that the trade unions have raised wages is wrong not only because any rises above the market level must penalise others but, more importantly, because the entire prosperity of society suffers when wages are determined by power and not competitive forces.[9]

The solution to this is not the abolition of the trade unions. The right to associate freely should be assured. And furthermore, everybody should have the right to strike, says Hayek, provided he breaks no contract and the law has not conferred any monopoly on his business.[10] But Hayek is convinced that nobody ought to have the right to force *others* to strike. He therefore sees no solution to the problem until the legal privileges of the trade unions, which allow them to force others to strike and which make them immune from many legal restraints, are ended.

Hayek concludes that perhaps the best solution would be to make all agreements in restraint of trade unenforceable in law. This would undoubtedly apply to closed shop agreements and other sources of coercion such as secondary strikes and boycotts. It would also, of course, apply to price fixing and other monopoly practices. But it is an oft-criticised deficiency of Hayek's writing on this subject that he does not offer any precise explanation of what activities constitute a 'restraint of trade'.

Other monopolies: We must recognise that many businesses which have achieved a monopoly or near-monopoly control over a market may have done so through simple superiority in serving the customer. Provided that other enterprises are free to build up capital and to challenge the position of a monopolist, his existence is not necessarily a cause for alarm or intervention.

The most likely case of a harmful monopoly will be one which has retained its power to protect its position even after the cause of its initial superiority has declined. For example, a monopoly has the power of discrimination in price; it can charge different rates to different customers. A common practice is to offer very low prices in regions where a potential competitor has arisen. But it is not certain that all price discrimination is harmful; and there are cases where a monopolist may be able to provide a better service *because* he can charge a higher price to one customer who can afford it and offer lower rates to others. So the problem is not solved by outlawing discrimination altogether.[11]

However, it is no doubt possible to detect cases where prices are manipulated in order to resist competition, and Hayek suggests that the task of policing this should be left to the potential competitors (who are more likely to be aware of market conditions than any government authority), by allowing them to sue for damages.

Cartels and other attempts to prevent competition, Hayek suggests, could be outlawed by the restraint of trade principle, in much the same way as the coercive practices of unions. Such general principle of law, he feels, would be more enforceable than the present attempts to disallow monopolies and cartels, which are fretted with exceptions, special cases and arbitrary decisions.[12]

Government monopoly over money: There is one last power of monopoly which governments have usually reserved for themselves. That is the creation and issuance of money. The great inflations of the 1970s forced Hayek to take a look at this subject, and he concluded rather remarkably that removing the government's privilege of being the sole creator of money would help prevent inflation and would ensure the existence of sound media for transactions.[13]

Although the issuance of money is normally thought to be an activity which must be done exclusively by the government, this has not always been so and need not be so.[14] At one time, governments no doubt played a useful role in certifying the weight and fineness of coins, but in the modern world where governments can inflate the currency over which they have monopoly powers of creation, this is no longer so. Indeed, the temptation to inflate, thereby gaining a temporary economic boost, is usually too strong to resist. So too is the advantage to the government that when prices rise, the debts it owes become smaller in real terms.

The cure for this unfortunate inflationary tendency is to allow private enterprises to issue their own competing currencies. The public would naturally choose the most reliable and stable, and the one least prone to inflation. Banks would probably issue currencies, backed by some assets to protect their stable value, and competition would prevent over-issuing. Individuals would be able to pay for goods in any currency which a supplier would accept, and both sellers and their customers would probably be well aware of any slight fluctuations from day to day through the newspapers. Hayek believes that under this regimen:

Government would then be deprived not only of one of the main means of damaging the economy and subjecting individuals to restrictions of their freedom but also of one of the chief causes of its constant expansion.[15]

If the government's own currency were respected and stable, of course, it may well be that people would stick largely with it; but the *threat* of competing currencies being issued would be sufficient to make sure that the inflationary tendency was kept in check.

Patents: The protection of personal property, which to Hayek is obviously a duty of government, is a concept that has been extended in recent times. The protection of monopoly powers by patents is an example. Hayek is doubtful about this privilege, arguing that it might not be the most effective form of reward for risk-bearing and investment in research, and that it causes difficulties in deciding what should be protected as 'property' and what should not.[16]

Regulation and certification: Attempts to regulate economic activity can sometimes be justified, but their costs must be weighed against their advantages. Regulations such as safety at work legislation cannot be justified by appeals to general principles; they are an imposition of certain values upon the market order, and therefore a form of coercion against the affected producers. But Hayek believes they may be justified if the benefits are large enough, and provided that the regulations are set down in advance and do not rely on vague discretionary powers.[17] Yet there is always one cost imposed by such regulations: the possible thwarting of new and beneficial development, which we can never calculate.

Certification and licensing of goods and services may be another thing which is needed to enable inexpert consumers to make rational choices between the alternatives offered, although it is not clear that only the government has the necessary stature to undertake these activities. Pure food laws, building regulations, minimum qualifications for doctors and lawyers, the safety of theatres, and other items fall into this

116

category. However, many of these controls would be made unnecessary by rules preventing people from pretending to qualifications they did not possess, provided that they had the right to appeal to an independent court in cases of dispute.[18]

The regulation of prices, however, is another matter. Prices depend on the circumstances of the time, and vary constantly as supply and demand conditions change. It is therefore impossible to fix a 'just' price which will serve efficient long-term production, and any such attempt to peg prices or wages will simply throw up a surplus or shortage before long. With the allocating powers of the price mechanism short-circuited, massive government intervention would be needed, and commands, not general rules, would govern economic activity.

THE WELFARE SYSTEM OF A FREE SOCIETY

Hayek does not rule out government action to deal with a comparatively recent development which is due to the emergence of a highly mobile open society: the existence of an increasing number of people who are no longer associated with kinship groups whose help they can count on in case of misfortune. These are the people who cannot make their own living in the market; the sick, the handicapped, the widows, orphans and the old are examples. According to Hayek, the best and fairest way of dealing with this problem is to have a minimum income, a floor which is a protection available to all against misfortune.

This does, of course, open Hayek up to charges that he is simply advocating 'social justice' with all its defects, and indeed, the mechanism he advocates is not easy to justify. However, he points out that the guarantee of a minimum income is a guarantee from which everyone benefits, like the guarantee of defence. It is undoubtedly a privilege, a special exemption from the rigours of the general rules of society, and it must be of limited application. But it may be necessary in the large modern society where an individual no longer has any claims over other members of the community into which he was born.[19]

Pensions: There is no reason why pensions, or any other benefit which can be provided by insurance, should be a monopoly of the government or even be provided by the government. 'Social insurance' has been assumed from the outset to be *compulsory* insurance by a state-controlled organisation. The justification for this, that it would be cheaper if everyone were protected by the same organisation, ignored the potential benefits from competition in the provision of services, and it has undoubtedly raised the costs of administering government-run pension schemes. And like so many 'social policies', the pensions system has become a vote-catching device aimed more at redistributing incomes than at achieving true insurance principles.

If we are determined to ensure that people should be protected against the needs of old age, the loss of a family breadwinner, or disability, then they can be required to make adequate provisions, because without that provision they would become a charge on the public.[20] We insist on compulsory insurance for motorists, not in their own interests but in the interests of other parties who might be injured by them, and this principle could be extended to pensions, health insurance, life insurance and unemployment protection. Presumably Hayek intends the minimum income guarantee to enable those suffering temporary misfortune to keep paying their premiums (if the misfortune is not already deriving them benefits on these policies). But there is of course no reason why this compulsory provision of insurance to some acceptable minimum level should be administered by the government; it would certainly be cheaper and more responsive to need if it could be done through existing insurance companies.

Health: Once again, there is a case for making health insurance compulsory, since those who did not insure themselves would become a public charge. But the case of health is interesting, because it shows up many of the reasons why a single level of 'fair' government provision would be wrong.[21]

The calls for a national health service with one level of treatment for all stem from the mistaken assumption that there is an objective 'need' for health which people have, making it unfair if some people cannot afford to attend to this objective 'need'. However, as in all things, human desires are very diverse, and some people are prepared to pay for more, or quicker, medical treatment than others deem necessary. There is almost no end to the number of tests a doctor can perform on a patient, or to the level of comfort or service which can be afforded him while under treatment. But even the richest man usually does not do all that could be done to protect his health, because he has other priorities and demands on his time. Only the individual, and not the government, can decide what level of testing or treatment is appropriate.

The foundation for a free health service, that the needs for medical care are objective and should be met in full, is therefore clearly mistaken. In any case, there is no reason why the provision of treatment or health insurance should be seen as a government monopoly.

Unemployment: Unemployment is a similar misfortune to ill health, and likewise does not require a compulsory state-run insurance scheme to protect individuals from its effects. Hayek's suggestion is to have genuine insurance against unemployment wherever practicable, allowing the different risks inherent in various trades to be reflected in the premiums paid. This has the supplementary advantage of distributing the costs of these risks to the industries concerned, helping the market process: the rising trades with a greater continuity of employment would be more attractive, but people would be discouraged from entering declining industries where unemployment was a greater risk and premiums were therefore higher.

Education: The case for compulsory education up to a certain level is twofold: firstly, we are exposed to less risk from our fellows if they share a basic knowledge with us; and secondly, democratic institutions are unlikely to work in an illiterate society.

There is therefore a case for government finance of some general education at least, but not for government management or monopoly of it. The educational voucher idea (proposed by

119

Milton Friedman) is endorsed by Hayek as a possible way of
making a public contribution to the costs of general education,
to which parents could add if they so desired. It gives parents a
choice of schools and avoids government control over so
important and potentially powerful a function as primary and
secondary education.[22]

As for higher education, there may be a case for financing it
publicly, in that academic research and development benefits
the whole community. But on the other hand there would
clearly be no case for financing, say, vocational training which
benefited the student far more than any other individual or
group.

Housing: The last of the services which are normally seen as
essential is housing, a service where governments have widely
interfered, but, says Hayek, usually to the detriment of those
needing houses.[23]

One example is rent restriction, originally introduced as an
emergency measure and maintained because it appears to keep
rents within the grasp of poorer people. But like all price fixing,
it drives resources away, and its primary result has been a
chronic housing shortage wherever it has been pursued. The
owner loses interest in protecting his unprofitable capital, and
houses fall into decay. People remain in houses that are too big
for them, further reducing the supply, and fewer people build
new houses for rent. Calls for more government intervention
mount as the shortage grows.[24]

Housing is therefore a classic case illustrating Hayek's
objection to Western welfare policies: not that they are
practised, but they are practised in ways which destroy the
market process and the liberal order.

CHAPTER SIX

The Constitution of a Liberal State

The effective limitation of power is the most important
problem of social order.[1]

HAYEK'S published works show a central and increasing
preoccupation with the problem of controlling the growth of
government. The problem which was raised in *The Road to
Serfdom* occupied much more of his attention in *The Constitution
of Liberty* and became the driving idea behind the three volumes
of *Law, Legislation and Liberty*, where he proposes a model
constitution for containing the powers of government
authorities. This deepening concern with the problem was
always a step ahead of the public's appreciation of it. Few in
1944 thought that moderate social engineering would ever lead
to a rise in arbitrary government; although welfare measures
had grown far beyond anyone's expectations in 1960, most
thought that they could be contained and improved; and even
though by the late 1970s the apparently unstoppable
momentum of the government sector was obvious, few had
solutions to offer.

The growth of government and its involvement in an ever
widening sphere of life might not be altogether unexpected in
countries where there are no limits to the absolute power of a
parliament or a monarch or dictator. But, says Hayek, even
those countries where there nominally exists a 'separation of
powers' have failed to resist it.[2] The principal reason, he
suggests, is a confusion of two different types of thing which are
both unfortunately called 'law' – that is, the general rules of
justice which enable a free society to grow and flourish without
any central direction, and the organisational rules of
authorities, aimed at achieving some particular social plan.
Because we call them all 'law', we suppose that every measure
of a government body has the same legitimacy, whereas in fact

it may be that many such resolutions conflict with the rules of just conduct. Even a constitutional separation of powers will therefore not contain the growth and arbitrary extension of government power if it does not limit the government to a certain *kind* of action, consistent with the general rules which are essential for the functioning of a free society. We must therefore remind ourselves of the crucial difference between the two types of 'law'.

THE TWO TYPES OF LAW

Hayek suggests several alternative descriptions for the two different types of law which he discerns.[3] The distinction suggested in the title of his trilogy, *the law* and *legislation*, is perhaps the easiest to use.

The law – rules of justice: The smooth operation of the social order is due to the fact not that it is planned, but that it is instead the outcome of individuals acting in certain regular ways. The rules we all follow enable us to take certain of the actions of others for granted, and therefore to co-operate with a measure of confidence. Rules which generate a functioning social order will allow one group to expand while others fail. The rules are therefore not the arbitrary commands of kings, commanders or legislators, but are discovered over a long period of time by an evolutionary process. In most cases, indeed, nobody will know all of the circumstances which caused one helpful rule to be followed and another disruptive or inadequate one to be dropped.

It is the attempt to express these general rules in words which is the purpose of legal theory. In the liberal view of society, the existence of these rules is prior to the attempt to write them down. The *law* is essentially discovered, not made. Even the impressive codes written down by Solon of Athens or Hammurabi of Babylon, says Hayek, were not attempts to 'give' their societies new laws, but were attempts to express clearly and unequivocally what the generally accepted laws, the commonly held rules of justice, actually were.

True *law* does command this important measure of agreement, because it has grown up in a society of free men.

Free men will commit themselves to following general rules and curbing some parts of their behaviour if it is conducive to the growth of a smooth order with the benefits that it brings. The law which grows up in this way applies equally to all, not distinguishing between people, whatever their differences. It therefore commands a wide measure of agreement, resting on general opinion of what is right and wrong, and not on a rather unlikely common will to bring about certain particular results.[4] For the achievement of particular results, even if they could be agreed upon, would require an authority to treat people differently in the pursuit of that aim.

The rules of justice are therefore not made by princes, but *discovered* by judges, and the long history of common law has been one of trying to discover these general rules which, when applied equally to all, will achieve a smooth social environment. Disputes will always arise, of course, as different people may disagree about the application of the rules in particular cases, or may find instances where one rule seems to conflict with another. This will require a judgement, which forms the precedent for similar cases in the future.

The purpose of the judge, therefore, is to preserve an order, not to achieve some particular result or to direct the resources of society to some particular end. The rules of justice which he helps to discover and refine are principles which tell everyone how to act, being good for all individuals both now and in the future, until they are replaced by others. They are abstract, not attempting to make any known individual or group play a part in achieving a known purpose, but to preserve an order of individuals who are unknown and who have many different private purposes.[5]

The judge cannot be concerned with the interests of specific groups, therefore, nor with the ambitions of public policy: His sole function is to determine, articulate and refine the rules of justice which will allow the preservation of the social order. In this sense a 'socialist judge' is a contradiction in terms, for a real judge can never be concerned with the political outcome of his decisions. His task is the purely technical one of resolving the uncertainties in an existing framework of rules of justice that is prior to the philosophies of any political movement.

Legislation – the rules of organisation: Ancient governments were principally occupied in the discovery of the law. Indeed, remarks Hayek, the ancient and mediaeval understanding was that a government could neither create nor abolish laws, for that would mean creating or abolishing justice itself, which is absurd.[6] Only in later mediaeval times did the idea of making new laws – *legislation* – begin to creep in. Thus began the establishment of parliament as a law-creating body, not a law-finding one, and the rule of law began to be replaced by the rule of men.

At this point the law-finding function of government began to get very mixed up with its administrative functions. Where a part of the resources of a nation is set aside to be administered by a government for the benefit of all, its activities clearly cannot be fully determined by general rules of just conduct. The resources which it controls are there to be marshalled towards particular purposes, and this marshalling will require an administrative organisation to achieve those aims. Much so-called 'law' is now administrative *legislation* of this type, designed to run the administrative machinery, not to preserve justice.[7]

The rules which facilitate the administration of the government machinery, however, do not always apply only to government servants. Raising taxes, for example, is an administrative measure which clearly affects everyone. The fact that such measures spilled out so widely constituted a potential threat to free men and encouraged the democratic ideal that both the rules of just conduct and the administration of government should be decided by representatives of the people.

Sadly, this concentrated the power of setting out clear and general rules of just conduct, the power of deciding the objectives of communal action, and the power to organise towards those objectives into the same hands. Soon, the distinction between rules of justice and administrative commands became blurred, and as it did so, the restraints upon government power fell away. As late as the seventeenth century it could still be debated whether a parliament could propose laws that were inconsistent with the principles of common law. Today, the powers of elected assemblies are allowed to extend into every corner of life.

Problems caused by the confusion about laws: The confusion about the two different kinds of 'law' has therefore contributed to the growth of government and the extension of its arbitrary powers in two ways. Firstly, the fact that all resolutions of elected assemblies are lumped together under the name of 'laws' gives administrative commands the false status of true law, the law of just conduct, with the aura of general acceptance and respect which that implies. Secondly, the same mistake leads to the assumption that the elected assembly has and should have just as much power in the determination of rules of justice as it has in the design and execution of administrative proposals. This in turn has encouraged the mistaken belief that society and the rules which enable it to function can be manipulated at will by human agencies in an attempt to re-design society.

Unfortunately, once legislators begin the conscious re-design of society to match their own ideas of utopia, there is no logical place to stop. There is no limit to the range, number and arbitrariness of the commands which could be issued in the pursuit of some particular ideal. And where an elected authority is not subject to any restraint in directing resources towards such objectives, it soon thinks of itself as 'running the country' as one would run a factory. When private property has thus become a datum of government administration, the question of whether government control over property (and therefore over all human life) is partial or complete is but a question of degree. Hayek has many time repeated his belief that:

It seems clear that a nominally unlimited ('sovereign') representative assembly must be progressively driven into a steady and unlimited extension of the powers of government.[8]

Such powers are hardly likely to make the relationships between men more predictable and thus generate an effective social order. Where what is 'just' is decided by parliaments and

125

not by a long process of discovery over many years, there are no limits to what might be proposed, whether it discriminates for or against particular groups, leaves important decisions to the discretion of government agencies, or even is retrospective in its effect. Such measures cannot even be criticised as 'unjust' if it is the elected governors who decide the measure of justice. So it appears that

To leave the law in the hands of elective governors is like leaving the cat in charge of the cream jug – there soon won't be any, at least no law in the sense in which it limits the discretionary power of government.[9]

DEMOCRACY AND THE RULE OF LAW

The fact that many governments which have grown to possess such large discretionary powers are nevertheless democratically elected draws Hayek into a reluctant analysis and criticism of the principles of democracy. The democratic and the liberal traditions agree that whenever some government action is required, the decision ought to be made by the majority. But the liberal tradition, in which Hayek places himself, sets firm limits to the powers which the majority can vote themselves, in order that majority rule is prevented from degenerating into a tyranny.

This view is not so strange, despite the tendency for 'democracy' to be used as a term of praise and any limit on it to be regarded with suspicion. It is indeed a laudible institution, says Hayek, but even the most ardent democrat would not argue for its unlimited extension. To extend the vote to infants, to residents of other countries, to the insane and to many other groups might be less than useful.[10] And similarly, the other way of extending democracy, to extend the range of issues voted on, is not always likely to be for the best. A majority cannot presume that there is no reasonable limit to its power, nor would anyone suppose that majority decisions are blessed with a higher, superindividual wisdom. Generally, they will be less wise than individual decisions, made with less thought of the consequences and a more sketchy consideration of the facts.[11]

Corruption of the democratic ideal: Although the institution of majority rule can therefore be a laudible one, it is wise to remember that its acceptance rests only on the benefits it brings:

Democracy is essentially a means, a utilitarian device for safeguarding internal peace and individual freedom. As such it is by no means infallible or certain.[12]

One common way in which an unlimited democracy can fail to deliver its promise of peace and freedom is by its becoming a prisoner of the conflicting pressures of sectional interest groups. The more power that an elected assembly has to distribute resources to certain groups and to tax others, the more is it likely to be the target for political pressure by organised lobbies. The voting powers of such groups will be used to support the politicians and policies which best protect their interests, and the package of policies proposed by any political party will be designed to attract the greatest support by attempting to give benefits and privileges to the widest range of such sectional groups. Even if a politician despises such an arrangement and wishes to sweep it away, he will still be a prisoner to it, since:

This legalised corruption is not the fault of the politicians; they cannot avoid it if they are to gain positions in which they can do any good.[13]

This relentless pressure to impose the wishes of the majority, or at least of a collection of sectional groups, in turn reduces the ability of politicians to think at all freshly about the politics and principles of a free society. For in such an environment:

The successful politician owes his power to the fact that he moves within the accepted framework of thought, that he thinks and talks conventionally. It would be almost a contradiction in terms for a politician to be a leader in the field of ideas. His task in a democracy is to find out what the opinions held by the largest number are, not to give currency to new opinions which may become the majority view in some distant future.[14]

It is clear, therefore, that many of the same forces which make majority rule such a praiseworthy institution lead it to be extended into inappropriate areas, such as the private sphere of individuals, at the expense of the principles of true justice. The

127

widespread belief that, because elected assemblies rest on the authority of the people, they should be free to pass whatever measures they deem appropriate, is clearly mistaken, for such freedom of parliament would mean oppression of the people[15] before too long. Some sort of limitation of powers is therefore essential:

We can either have a free Parliament or a free people. Personal freedom requires that all authority is restrained by long-run principles which the opinion of the people approves.[16]

The constitution and the rule of law: Undoubtedly the development of constitutional government has helped in the containment of arbitrary power. This form of government makes current legislation subject to a higher law, and works by the separation of powers, so that the legislative assembly is different from the body which judges the constitutionality of its actions.

Yet Hayek wants to go much further than this. Powers may be separated but not necessarily limited, and a constitution may not necessarily prove effective in curbing them. The task is not to separate powers, but to contain them, for

The chief evil is unlimited government, and nobody is qualified to wield unlimited power.[17]

Keeping the powers of government within the limits of the principles of justice, therefore, is more than simply constitutionalism. This *rule of law* requires that the coercive powers of the government may not be used except in accordance with general rules; it requires that the rules should be known and certain; it requires that people should be treated equally, that the law should be no respecter of persons; it requires independent judges, unmotivated by political ambitions; and it requires that a private domain of action and property should be protected.[18]

We can now appreciate why a true separation of powers has never in fact been achieved, because the power of deciding the rules of just action and the power of directing government have always been combined in the same representative assemblies. In consequence, the ultimate powers of governments have never been 'under law', because they themselves decide the 'law', and can make whatever 'law' they want for the particular tasks they desire to undertake.

A MODEL CONSTITUTION

Hayek believes that a constitutional bastion against the erosion of the rule of law would require two entirely different chambers of government, with a different composition and not operating in collusion or even deciding the same kinds of issues. One body would be charged with the task of setting down the rules of just conduct, general rules of action that are followed only to preserve the social order and not to achieve specific targets. The other body would be charged with the administration of government services; while the functions it might undertake would not be defined, its coercive powers would be limited by the rules of justice laid down by the first.[19]

The legislative assembly: Hayek wishes to give as much independence as possible to the first body, the one charged with setting out the rules of just conduct. The existence of factions or parties within it would be entirely inappropriate, for it should be concerned only with justice and not with the promotion of a particular political ideal. He suggests that this independence might be achieved by electing its members for long periods, after which they would not be re-eligible, but would assume honorific positions as lay judges. During their tenure, therefore, they would not be dependent on party support nor concerned about their personal future.

Hayek also feels that the members of this body should be people whose contemporaries respect them, and who reflect prevailing opinion about the standards of right and wrong. He therefore suggests that they should be elected by asking each group of people of the same age, once in their lives, say at age 45, to select from their midst representatives to serve for fifteen years.[20]

The result would be an assembly of men and women who were aged between 45 and 60, one-fifteenth of whom would be replaced each year. The assembly would therefore mirror that part of the population who were experienced and mature, but still in their best years, and it would be immune from the pressures of political parties or sectional interests. Furthermore, its average age would still be lower than that of most present-day elected assemblies. Hayek believes that:

such a system of election by the contemporaries, who are always the best judges of a man's ability, as a sort of prize awarded to 'the most successful member of the class', would come nearer producing the ideal of the political theorists, a senate of the wise, than any system yet tried. It would certainly for the first time make possible a real separation of powers, a government under the law and an effective rule of law.[21]

The governmental assembly: The rules of just conduct laid down by the legislative assembly would limit the powers of the other body, but within this limit, the governmental assembly would have total control in organising the apparatus of government and deciding about the use of the material and other resources entrusted to it.

The problem of taxation shows usefully how this constitutional arrangement would operate. Taxation is a coercive activity, and so the principle on which taxes were raised would have to be defined by general rules laid down by the legislative assembly. Yet the size of the amount to be raised would be a governmental matter. Except where the beneficiaries of a particular measure could be identified and charged (such as a roads tax), the costs of government activities would fall upon the members of the governmental assembly and their constituents in accordance with principles which they were powerless to alter. There could therefore be no way of eliciting support for new expenditure on the excuse that the burden could be shifted onto someone else's shoulders.

This arrangement could certainly still provide whatever collective goods the majority were willing to pay for; but it would be unable to deflect the stream of incomes produced by the market for the benefit of particular interest groups. And it would require the individual to contribute, and to behave with respect to others, only in accordance with common rules. It could not require particular people to act in particular ways or to serve some particular purpose of government.

The constitutional court: Although the distinction between the powers of the two assemblies is reasonably clear, there would in practice always arise many difficulties, and these could be worked out only through a special court.

The most usual issue, a conflict in competence between the two assemblies, would make it appropriate to have professional judges as members of the court, and possibly former members of the two assemblies.

The constitution is also an interesting construct. Hayek's suggestion is that it should allocate and restrict powers, but should not prescribe positively how these powers are to be used. It would define only the general attributes which enforceable rules of just conduct must possess in order to be laid down by the legislative assembly; that is, it would define the extent of the protected domain which the individual could enjoy with certainty and without the interference of any discretionary powers, and it would lay down the necessary conditions of the rule of law.

Sense and Sorcery in the Social Sciences

The great differences between the characteristic
methods of the physical sciences and those of the social
sciences explain why the natural scientist who turns to
the work of the professional students of social
phenomena so often feels that he has got among a
company of people who habitually commit all the
mortal sins which he is most careful to avoid, and that
a science of society conforming to his standards does
not yet exist.[1]

HAVING been raised in a family of natural scientists, and
himself having a sympathy with and understanding of the aims
and methods of the natural sciences, it was natural that Hayek
should react strongly when he turned to the study of social
phenomena and found that the methods of the natural sciences
were being misapprehended and uncritically applied to
problems for which they were entirely inappropriate. This
reaction was manifested in *Scientism and the Study of Society* and a
number of essays since.[2]

It is not surprising that students of social phenomena should
wish to emulate the undoubted successes of the physical
sciences. The progress of the physical sciences in modern times
has exceeded all expectations, and has enabled us to predict
and control our physical environment to an astonishing degree,
and to manufacture and enjoy new benefits which add greatly
to our comfort. Yet the confidence in the unlimited power of
science, says Hayek, is all too often based on a false belief that
scientific method is merely the application of a ready-made
investigative technique.[3] In seeking to offer ways of controlling
society, as the physical scientist offers methods of controlling
the physical world, social scientists have imitated the form
rather than the substance of scientific technique. And because
of the momentous consequences which can follow from any

attempt to control society, there is reason to be apprehensive about many assertions of social scientists which may have the *appearance* of being scientific but which result from a misunderstanding of the crucial differences between physical and social phenomena.

THE DIFFERENCES BETWEEN NATURAL AND SOCIAL SCIENCES

The natural scientist aims for objectivity in his studies. He stands outside the physical object, the chemical reaction, the plant or the animal he is investigating, and attempts to describe its behaviour in an unbaised way, without his own feelings and prejudices entering into the matter. The way in which human beings see the world, and the feelings they have about it, is not what interests him, for his task is to show that our uninformed view of the world is often very feeble and inconsistent.

The scientist is interested in the relationships between natural objects, not in the relationships between men and natural objects. For example, human beings might think that ice and water were two entirely different materials, since their appearance and texture are so very different. But some simple scientific tests (such as allowing the ice to melt) show that, despite their appearances, these things are ultimately made of the same material.

Or again, the scientist gets outside our inadequate human view of the world by showing how apparently similar things can be distinguished. A series of white powders, for example, might appear identical to a human being. Their touch, taste, smell and other qualities might be indistinguishable. But the scientist can show that they are in fact quite different by performing chemical tests on them. By looking at the relationships between the powders and other chemicals, and disregarding our fallible sensations, he is able to show us something new about the way the world is made up and works.[4]

This approach is particularly useful. It helps us to predict the behaviour of natural objects, because the scientist can trace regular relationships between things which we previously thought were unrelated or chaotic. And it helps us to distinguish things which might appear the same superficially, but which have important differences and can therefore be put to different uses. Hence the impact which scientific developments have had over our lives.

So successful has this scientific approach been, enabling us to control and shape our world with far more certainty than would have been possible if we had relied on the naïve view of our senses, that many students of social affairs have naturally attempted to apply the same procedure to their own fields. Many of them insist that the only correct way to study society is to observe and measure what societies actually do. Any enquiry into what people think about their societies, or *why* they act in the ways they do, is seen as unscientific because it brings personal motives and values into a study which should be completely objective. The purpose of studying society, on this view, is the same as the purpose of studying natural objects: to change and improve our view of them, not to re-state old views.

The distinctive needs of the social sciences: Hayek insists that this attempt to apply the methods of the natural sciences uncritically to social study is a grave error, which he calls *scientism*. It is so because the social sciences deal with the relations between men and men (and men and things), not with the relations between things and things. When we try to discount people's attitudes about their society, and the motives which make them behave in certain ways, then we have eliminated everything which is important in the formation and operation of human societies, and therefore made our social study quite impossible and pointless.

It is perfectly possible to describe the behaviour of human beings 'mechanistically'. Their reactions to physical stimuli, for example, can be investigated and charted. But this often tells us less about the world than we could know if we took their motivations into account. For example, an archaeologist may unearth a stone that appears to have been deliberately fashioned. The only way he can discover whether it was made or whether it is a natural formation is to attempt to reconstruct the motivations of the men who might have made it. What purpose it might have had to its creator, and how he might have fashioned it, are crucial questions if we are to understand what the stone really is. The purposes of men *cannot* be left out, as the natural scientist might wish to leave them out.[5]

As a further example, consider the different tools and instruments which we use today, such as hammers or barometers. They can indeed be described mechanistically, in purely physical terms. But to do so would miss out the very reason for their existence: that they are used by men for certain purposes. In physical terms there is almost no relationship between a steamhammer and an ordinary hammer, so if human motivation is not taken into account, they would be described as two very different things. But, of course, we know that they are linked in an important way, in that they both serve the same general purpose.

What is true of the purposes men have for things is even more true of relations between men, for such relationships cannot be described at all in the objective terms of the physical sciences, but only in terms of human attitudes and beliefs. Economics is particularly rich in examples of this. Money, for instance, cannot be defined in terms of physics or chemistry. The fact that money is usually made from printed paper or round disks of metal is neither here nor there to an economist; he is interested only in the value which people put on it and the various commodities it can be exchanged for. No physical descriptions of iron or wool, nor all the scientific knowledge we could gain about them, would ever explain the price of iron or wool; only information about what the people dealing in them think about those commodities would yield an explanation.

The raw materials we must analyse in economics or in any other social science are therefore not physical objects, capable of an objective description without reference to human purposes. The raw materials of the social sciences *are* men, and things as they *appear* to men. Any attempt to explain the behaviour of men in groups without reference to the attitudes and motives of the men themselves is therefore bound to fail.

Further complications: Even this is an oversimplification. While people's *views* about things and about other men are the true raw materials of the social sciences, these same people form their own popular theories about how and why people act. These, of course, can be completely mistaken, and supposing them to be facts is a constant danger because they can be as inaccurate as the naïve views that ice and water are not the same material or that different white chemical powders are in fact identical. The purpose of social science is to reconstruct these popular images, not to build a new theory on top of them.

We have therefore to distinguish between ideas which *motivate* people to behave in certain ways and ideas which people use to *explain* to themselves how they behave. For example, the views which people hold about a commodity will determine its price. But people might form a variety of explanations about why prices change and how value is determined. Or again, the beliefs and opinions which prompt people to manufacture and bring their goods to market time and time again are entirely different from their theories about the economic system of which they are a part and to which their activity contributes.

Unfortunately, in his attempt to keep away from the personal ideas which motivate people and to be as objective as the natural scientist, the social scientist often confuses popular explanations with facts. Even such concepts as 'society', 'capitalism', or 'the economic system' are really only popular explanations; they are generalisations and rough theories which the social scientist has to improve on, not treat as if they were objective facts.

In particular, the social scientist must be especially wary of the popular belief that social phenomena are deliberately designed. If the results of all human action were deliberately intended, then to explain any result we would need only look to the science of psychology. The fact that human actions often have unintended consequences is the very thing which makes social science necessary. How people's valuation of things is translated into prices, which in turn cause people to steer resources in one direction rather than another, is the sort of question which social science has to answer, even though the way in which resources are steered is not due to the deliberate planning or intent of any individual. The object of social theory is thus to discover why people act the way they do with respect to each other, why they co-operate, what influences their choices, and how these choices combine to produce a particular result. These are questions which many social theorists, being concerned to do without any mention of human motives in their study, are completely unable to answer.

Discussion of Hayek's views on the social sciences is complicated because they underwent a significant change after the early 1940s, when his initial work on the subject was done. He was originally of the view that the methods of the social and natural sciences were completely different, and that any attempt to apply the methods of one to the other was mistaken.

However, in the meantime, Sir Karl Popper produced a convincing explanation of the essential unity of all scientific method, which forced Hayek to reconsider. According to Popper, all science is a process of prediction and testing: a theory is advanced, subjected to scrutiny, and rejected if it is found wanting. The physicist, for example, predicts the future behaviour of physical objects on the basis of his theories about how they work. If his predictions are correct, they support his theory (although they do not necessarily prove that he is correct, since other explanations might be possible). If his predictions are incorrect, then the theory is adequately refuted.

This method characterises good social science just as much as good physics. Indeed, it is the test of the 'scientific' nature of social science that it uses this method, that it makes predictions that are in principle refutable by future facts, and that its theories are tested against reality and abandoned where lacking.

Hayek's later writings therefore come down to a set of guidelines for what a good theory in the social sciences would look like, rather than a blanket criticism of all attempts by social scientists to be 'scientific' by emulating other disciplines. His warning to students of society is that they should be careful to understand what they are trying to predict, and that even though the basic principles of scientific method might still apply to them, social sciences have important characteristics of their own.

THE ENEMIES OF A GENUINE SOCIAL SCIENCE

Hayek points to a number of specific mistakes which arise when this special characteristic of social science is not understood. They are all still common mistakes, although the efforts of Hayek and others have begun to drive many of them out of respectable studies of society.[6]

Behaviourism: Behaviourism is an attempt to dispense with our subjective knowledge of the human mind, a denial of the tool of introspection in explaining the behaviour of others. It seeks for relationships between physical stimuli and behaviour, rejecting explanations in terms of intention, motivation or purpose.

This, says Hayek, is a very inconsistent theory, because even the stimuli which we take to be objective might not seem the same to all people. Someone who is tired, or under the influence of a certain drug, might perceive (and react to) a certain stimulus differently from someone else. So in attempting to study anyone's reaction to a stimulus, we have to admit that what seems objectively similar to us might appear different to others. It is *impossible* to exclude a subjective element.

And as we have seen, things which may be physically very different, such as an ordinary hammer and a steamhammer, or the written word and its spoken equivalent, may 'mean' the same thing to a human being and may elicit the same reaction. To get any understanding at all, therefore, about how the human mind works and why human beings react in particular ways to particular situations, we have to use our personal knowledge of how we would react in those circumstances: that is, we can never be completely impersonal and objective if we want to understand what is really important about human behaviour.

False measurement: This misplaced thirst for objectivity often leads social scientists into the blind measurement of social phenomena. In the natural sciences, this procedure has led to many successes, and so measurement is often thought of as the hallmark of scientific activity.

In the social sciences, however, its whole purpose is lacking.

A society is not a system of quantities, but a system of relationships between individuals. Measurement in this context cannot help but assign numerical values to things which are irrelevent aspects of social phenomena. The treatment of social relationships in numerical terms serves only to obscure the things which are truly important in the workings of social groups.

Collectivism: In terms of scientific method, collectivism is the grouping together of things which may be very different, and treating them as if they were unitary wholes. This is very common in popular speculation, where it is supposed that *society* or *the economy* is somehow a unitary whole and that there is some 'object' to which these words refer. This in turn suggests that the groups act in a unified way, as if invested with a single mind.

It is easy to see that this can lead to great mistakes. When we say that *France* exports so much wine, that the *steel industry* employs so many men, or that *capitalism* rose, flourished and decayed, we are not talking about particular unitary things. It is just our shorthand way of referring to the individual wine exporters of France, the various firms in the steel industry, and the people, companies, opinions, market relations and ideas which comprise the concept of capitalism.[7] Problems begin to arise when we forget that we are using a shorthand description and treat these notions as if they really existed as concrete wholes. Firstly, we tend to think of them as if they were people and to suppose that they will react with a singleness of purpose: calls for *society* to do this or that are legion, for example, despite the fact that society is not a person nor even a deliberate organisation which can do particular things. And secondly, our understanding of these concepts is reduced because we overlook the relationships between people which are central to them. It would be impossible to understand the functioning of *the price system*, for example, without considering the individual values of the people in the marketplace whose actions make up the workings of that system. And to speak of *society* as if it were a unitary whole obscures all the complex relationships of money, punishments, crime, language, use of tools and many others which we have to understand before we can say anything about the overall pattern of activity which these relationships form.

Statistics: A particular consequence of this methodological collectivism is the assumption that statistical methods can tell us something about the nature of social structures.

An example from the field of linguistics shows us how unlikely this is to be true. No amount of statistical analysis of the use of words, for instance, will tell us anything about the structure of language. Although words are used systematically, mathematical information about them does not help us to understand the complex system of grammar which governs their use. The same is true in society, says Hayek: individuals are bound together by a web of relationships, and no statistical analysis of individuals will enable us to begin to understand those relationships.

To understand the impotence of statistics in the field of social studies, we have to recognise their correct application. Statistics summarise the attributes of collections of individuals. They assume that the individuals under study are not systematically connected, so that any sample from a large population would be representative. Far from dealing with structures of relationships, statistics *deliberately ignore* any relationships which might exist between the individuals under investigation.

Most economic statistics, such as figures about price changes, national income analysis and so on, are an attempt to apply statistical techniques to unsuitable data, data which are connected by human values and relationships. Because these relationships, the deciding factors, are overlooked by statistical analysis, no useful information is likely to come from the statistical approach. The most it can do is to give us some measurements of past events, which (if the data are legitimately measurable) may be very interesting as historical records, but which can never point out generalisations that can be extended into the future.

Historicism: Historicism is a doctrine much popularised by Marx, which rests on mistaken principles. The first is that there are no general laws of social behaviour which apply in different societies or historical epochs. The second is that the only general law is a law of history, which shows how one historical epoch turns into the next, such as how feudalism turns into mercantilism, then industrial capitalism, and so on. This view, which was once very prevalent, has today been almost entirely driven out of social studies, so only a brief summary is needed here.[8]

The first historicist principle argues that a price or a monopoly, say, is not the same in feudal England or ancient Egypt as it is today, and so cannot be compared. This, of course, is nonsense, because we do perceive regular arrangements of things in different societies and in different historical times which we recognise to be similar, and which we can discuss. The exact prices which prevailed at a particular time depend on the circumstances of the moment; but in trying to explain them, we use exactly the same theory as we would today.

The second principle is used by historicists to show that history is moving 'inevitably' in some direction or to some particular end (with Marx it was communism), usually an end which the historicist happens to favour. This is of course a collectivist view and possesses all the faults and blindness of collectivism. It presumes that men are 'shaped' by 'society' and cannot escape their historical fate. But since 'society' is not a concrete object it does not shape anyone. The relations between men make up 'society', not the other way round.

The false assumption of deliberate design: The inaccurate use of the word 'purpose' can also lead social scientists into difficulties. For the word 'purpose', strictly speaking, implies the existence of someone who is deliberately aiming at a result. If we use it in the study of social phenomena, therefore, we might mistakenly conclude that social institutions are deliberately designed.

It can sometimes be very useful to ask, for example, what the 'purpose' of something like a body organ is. We know that it has not been deliberately designed, but we are interested in what its function is with respect to the whole body. Similarly, when we ask the 'purpose' of a custom, tradition or other social

141

structure, we must not suppose that someone is using it to promote a deliberate end. Nevertheless, social institutions (such as the price mechanism) often act *as if* they were consciously designed, even though they are not.

This mistake often leads people to suppose that human institutions are deliberately fashioned and that social structures have been deliberately built. This suggests that we can rebuild them to our specifications, which is a recipe for disaster, because we have not built these structures and usually understand very little about their 'purpose' and importance.

Social engineering: The most attractive feature of any science is that it enables us to shape the world, and so it is understandable that social scientists have also striven for this power. Unfortunately, the things which the mechanical engineer and the social engineer have to deal with are, once again, completely different in nature, which makes the task of the social engineer impossible.

The data which engineers have to compute when designing a new type of engine, for example, are usually well known. The mechanics of engines are well established, and the engineer can calculate how much power he will obtain from a given mix of fuel and machinery. But the application of engineering techniques to society assumes that the social engineer is similarly blessed with complete information about the things he is designing, when this is clearly not the case.

To decide on the most efficient allocation of resources, the planner has to consider their scarcity and alternative uses. The scarcity of capital, for example, is reflected in the rate of interest. But if the social planner is not prepared to accept information about capital scarcity in this abridged form, he will have to try in every instance to go back to be various uses for capital, investigate its availability in various forms, and then try to work out its most appropriate use. He needs to acquire the same complete knowledge of society that the mechanical engineer possesses about the mechanics of engines. But the information which has to be collected and concentrated for social planning is, of course, so fragmentary and individual, so vast in scope, that no planner could collect nor process it.

Because social structures are not based on a central collection of information, but on the separate knowledge of many people, the values they hold and the relationships which link them, social orders differ markedly from deliberate, planned organisations. The purpose of social science is not to suggest that we have the ability to engineer society when in fact we do not, but to demonstrate where lie the limits of our conscious control. We are part of a complex social process, one which has evolved to be far beyond the powers of the human mind to control. Failure to understand this explains most of the errors prevalent in the study of society.

THE LIMITS OF THE SOCIAL SCIENCES

If the social studies are to be considered as true sciences at all, then they must follow the generally accepted rules of scientific method: that is, they must produce theories which enable as to predict future events, theories which can be rejected if the predictions are false. A major part of Hayek's writings on the social sciences has been an attempt to discover whether such theories are actually possible in the study of social phenomena, or whether social events are impossible to predict by their very nature.

Hayek's later writings break away from the tradition of his colleagues in the 'Austrian School' of economics and social study. The traditional Austrian opinion is that no social events are possible to predict, and that the claim of economics and other social studies to be scientific is therefore fraudulent. But in his later works, Hayek argued that although specific social or economic events (such as the levels of prices in the stock market) cannot be predicted, other more general patterns of events (such as the tendency for shortages to occur when prices are controlled) certainly can be. The social sciences therefore *can* be called true sciences, although the scope of their theorising is limited.

To help understand this argument, it is perhaps wise to consider briefly the earlier position of Hayek and his Austrian colleagues before going on to discuss it more fully.

The early Hayek and the Austrians: The traditional Austrian approach even today, and Hayek's early belief, is that social and natural phenomena are two very different things in terms of complexity.

Despite the fact that many people think the subject-matter of science is very complex, this is not really so. The scientist investigates the world by leaving out as many confusing variables as possible, and trying to discover the relations between abstract 'ideal' objects under 'ideal conditions'. The mechanical laws of the physicist, for example, are therefore rather simple: only a few variables need to be inserted into a few key equations in order to predict the movements of physical objects.

In society, it is different. It takes a very much larger number of variables to describe the workings of even the simplest biological system or response, and to describe society would require a multitude of variables. Society is a complex arrangement of complex relationships between individuals who are themselves complex. And the problem is not just one of calculation, which a good computer could sort out. On the contrary, some of the variables we need in order to predict the structure of a society can never be known to us. Those key variables are the motivations of individuals, motives which are known only to themselves (and sometimes not understood properly even by them). These motives change, depending on time and circumstances and the opportunities which arise. But it would be essential to be able to predict such things at the individual level if we were ever to build a science of society. And since we cannot, then social science is impossible.

A simple example will help, although it is not Hayek's. If a Martian came down to earth, he might notice that at 8:35 a.m. each morning a tube of metal containing hundreds of people travels down a pair of metal rails from Oxford to London. He might formulate the theory that this will continue to happen regularly. For many weeks his theory might be supported by the events. But suppose that one day the metal tube did not travel: what would he think? How could his theory explain the fact? It could not, of course. Only when we understand that this tube is a train, that it carries people who want to get to London

144

and that it is driven by a man with motives of his own can we begin to understand what is happening at all. Only then can we suggest explanations such as the driver being ill or having to attend a funeral. In other words, an understanding of his motives is essential to understanding the workings of his world. Where his actions affect the motives and behaviour of others, they could be of major significance. Hence the absolute necessity of starting from the level of individual motivations when studying society.

But in the Austrian view, and in Hayek's earlier works, such motives can never be understood. And because social phenomena depend entirely upon the motives of the individuals who make up those phenomena, we can never fashion a reliable 'science' of society.

Hayek's later position: Hayek later came to believe that the methods of the natural sciences might be appropriate to the social sciences, although the events which we could hope to predict are much more limited in the latter fields. But while social science, correctly pursued, cannot hope to predict much more than general patterns of activity, what it predicts can nonetheless be very important.

Hayek's analysis is a distinctive treatment of the subject, and starts from the apparently unpromising position that social phenomena are indeed impossible to reduce to a few simple formulae. The scientist may well be able to simplify the physical world and banish unnecessary and confusing variables. But such simplification is impossible in the social sciences, for many of the structures of social life are necessarily complex. Competition, for example, depends upon there being large numbers of people in the market. Any attempt to simplify the process and extract a few key variables would ignore the very point which makes competition useful, that it operates only when large numbers of people come together for trade. Social phenomena are bound to be *complex* phenomena.[9]

If we devise some simple theory about the workings of a complex structure, it is bound to be inadequate. No manageable theory of competition, for example, will tell us about the behaviour of any particular competing individual, or enable us to predict what he will supply at what price at any specified time.

And yet, says Hayek, it may be possible to predict broad *patterns* of social events, even though we do not know which individuals will be acting to make up that pattern.

Hayek likens this prediction of patterns to someone describing the patterns on a carpet in that another person would instantly recognise the carpet from the description of the pattern, even though he may not have been told what the colour of the pattern was, how large it was, or what the individual strands of wool looked like. Or again, to take another example, when a radioactive isotope with a half-life of a hundred years is left to decay, we can be confident that in fifty years' time half of the radioactive atoms will have become inert, although we can never predict *which ones* will do so. We can predict the pattern of events, but we can never predict the behaviour of individual atoms, just as in society we can predict patterns of social phenomena but not the actions of any individual, nor any particular event.

Human beings are not like computers: almost any event in a person's life may have some unpredictable effect on any of his future actions, making it impossible to know precisely how he will behave, even *if* it were possible to know all the events which have occurred to him. So we can expect no simple regularities in human behaviour such as we might find in the behaviour of physical objects. Even if we knew a great deal about all of the people who operated in a particular market, for example, we would never be able to predict the prevailing price of the goods they bought and sold, because of the traders' individual complexity and the complexity of the relations between them, the way they value goods and how they behave towards others. No economist has been able to make a fortune by buying or selling commodities on the basis of his scientific prediction of future prices!

For this reason, economics and other social sciences are limited to describing kinds of *patterns* which will appear if certain conditions are satisfied. Despite the fact that this seems to offer very little to the social scientist, it may nevertheless be testable and valuable. If we predict that under certain conditions a certain pattern, yielding a maximisation of some variable, will emerge, then we can create the conditions required and see if the pattern occurs, even though we may be ignorant of the special circumstances which will determine the precise arrangement which will be manifested.

According to Hayek, the social sciences can never aim at the prediction of specific events, therefore, but they can help us to explain and understand the mechanisms which will produce patterns or orders of a certain kind, and this can be a very important tool in indicating what actions are desirable, or even if no action is desirable, to establish such patterns. And the legitimate study of social phenomena should also tell us of the instances where the method of the natural sciences is inappropriate, that is, in the naïve and futile attempt to discover simple regularities in complex phenomena which will make possible the deliberate manipulation of the detailed operation of the social world.

Hayek's analysis of the theory of complex phenomena and his demonstration that social theories can have the status of scientific theories (even though their power to predict is very limited) is undoubtedly a valuable one if it indeed helps us to explain and understand the conditions which will produce the kinds of social phenomena or economic progress that we want to achieve. But it must be said that Hayek's analysis is not completely satisfying, for he can give no clear limit of where the boundary is between legitimate theorising and hopeless, unfounded speculation. At one end, we know from him that the prediction of specific prices or actual quantities traded on any day is impossible. At the other, we know that broad pattern prediction is justifiable. But there seems to be no firm test for all the things in between which do not fall into the category of particular events or the category of broad patterns. Where does the boundary lie?

No doubt as the social sciences progress, and the social scientists learn which kinds of theories will predict classes of events with any accuracy and which will not, the boundary between the scientifically predictable and the unavoidably unknowable will be discovered. Hayek's achievement is to remind social scientists that there *is* a boundary, a barrier to scientific knowledge of society, somewhere; and to plead with them to be humble about the sort of predictions they can hope to achieve.

THE INTELLECTUALS AND SOCIALISM

These limitations in method and use of social science may well be understood by the more thorough practitioners of the art. They will make names for fine scholarship or find other routes to positions of high status and influence. But there is a much larger class of individuals who are unable or unwilling to appreciate the limits of social studies; for them, the creed that our advancing knowledge of society makes it possible to reconstruct the social world (as the natural scientists have reconstructed the physical world) is a source of attraction and status.

This creed finds itself particularly well represented, says Hayek, among intellectuals.[10] To him, intellectuals are not original thinkers, but the purveyors of second-hand ideas, including journalists, authors, teachers, ministers, publicists, artists and so on. Their reputation depends upon their being accepted by their colleagues, and being one step ahead of the prevailing climate of opinion, although not too far ahead. It is they who explore the application of old ideas to new areas, creating new errors, like the false application of the methods of natural science to the social sciences. Because they are communicators of ideas, these errors are quickly spread.

The intellectual, however, resents the apparent shackles which proper method seems to place on his ideas. If he ignores the limitations, or does not understand them, he can gain the respect of others by applying his mind to the utopian reconstruction of society. He is more attracted by the prospects for reform than he is restrained by methodological difficulties, which seem to him like mere technicalities which more research will eventually overcome.

The very best minds, who recognise this error, follow the rigorous path of academic pursuits because they enjoy it for its own sake. But those who are left, the second-best minds but the best of the intellectuals, are more interested in material reward. Being attracted by the prospects of social reform, they naturally assume that social institutions can be manipulated by their intelligent efforts; and after all, it is the intellectuals who would be the manipulators in a planned society, which must be an added attraction. Hence they tend to fall into a socialist conception of society, the mistaken belief that it can be shaped to conform to a common hierarchy of human values.

The concept of the society which is based on rational planning and scientific principles is a powerful ideal which captures the mind of the young. Against it, non-socialist thinkers often find themselves without much to offer. Their rejection of the sweeping social changes planned by utopian socialists unfortunately tends to make them seek shelter in the more comfortable and constant world of conservatism, even though this can hardly be described as an inspiring doctrine, and even though it relies upon the same use of power to impose its values as the socialist does to impose his. Hayek is therefore very sceptical about the reliance on conservatism as an antidote to socialist planning, and says of it:

Conservatism, though a necessary element in any stable society, is not a social program; in its paternalistic, nationalistic, and power-adoring tendencies it is often closer to socialism than true liberalism; and with its traditionalistic, anti-intellectual, and often mystical propensities it will never, except in short periods of disillusionment, appeal to the young and all those others who believe that some changes are desirable if this world is to become a better place.[11]

Does the liberal then have any ideals which he can hold up as the motivating principles for those who want to see the development of a better society? At first sight, the prospects look bleak.

Utopian socialist theory is almost impossible to fault on the grounds of practicality, because its adherents tend to assume that mere practical difficulties can be overcome; Hayek, however, shows that they can, in fact, *never* be overcome. The programme offered by the liberal social thinker must therefore be much more limited, and tends to be less inspiring. The liberal must remember the practicalities of the issue: he is dealing with social institutions which have a life of their own, and which do not respond well to our simplistic attempts to reform them. His ambition is to improve the working of existing social forces, forces which have arisen through a long period of evolution to serve complex functions which we can often hardly guess at. His task is to discover and create the conditions under which this system of forces is most likely to appear and work for the benefit of us all.

But the task of the liberal need not be entirely thankless. He does in fact have an attractive ideal to aim at, just like the socialist, and with the added benefit that his ideal rests on practicalities whereas the socialist ideal rests on errors. Hayek sees the challenge in this way:

> We must make the building of a free society once more an intellectual adventure, a deed of courage. What we lack is a liberal Utopia, a programme which seems neither a mere defence of things as they are nor a diluted kind of socialism, but a truly liberal radicalism which does not spare the susceptibilities of the mighty (including the trade unions), which is not too severely practical and which does not confine itself to what appears today as politically possible. . . Unless we can make the philosophic foundations of a free society once more a living intellectual issue, and its implementation a task which challenges the ingenuity and imagination of our liveliest minds, the prospects of freedom are indeed dark. But if we can regain that belief in the power of ideas which was the mark of liberalism at its best, the battle is not lost.[12]

Since those words were written in 1949, the battle has undoubtedly turned in favour of the liberals. From being an unexciting doctrine which largely defended the *status quo*, liberalism has become a radical new vision of a better world. Its implementation has indeed challenged the ingenuity and the imagination of a large number of the finest minds of recent years. Today, the prospects for freedom are brighter than they have been for a long time, a change which must be attributed in great measure to the better understanding of the principles of the free society that the modern world has been given by Friedrich Hayek.

Notes

Introduction: Hayek's life and work

1. *The Political Order of a Free People*, page 152. (For full bibliographic information on Hayek's works cited in the text, see the *Select bibliography* below.)

2. The word 'liberal' is used here as Hayek uses it, in the classical English sense and not the modern American sense.

3. A useful brief assessment of Hayek's importance in this regard can be found in the opening pages of Norman P. Barry, *Hayek's Social and Economic Philosophy* (London: Macmillan, 1979).

4. The condensed version, which appeared in the *Reader's Digest*, earned Hayek's praise for its skilful abridgement of his text: 'It is inevitable that the compression of a complex argument to a fraction of its original length produces some oversimplification, but that it was done without distortion and better than I could have done it myself is a remarkable achievement.' See note 3 to '*The Road to Serfdom* after Twelve Years' in *Studies in Philosophy, Politics and Economics*, page 218.

5. Hayek has talked about his relationship with Mises in a lecture, 'Coping with Ignorance', transcribed in *Imprimis* Vol.7, No.7, (Hillsdale, Michigan: Hillsdale College, July 1978).

A distinguished review of Mises's work can be found in Israel M. Kirzner (ed.), *Method, Process and Austrian Economics* (Lexington, Massachusetts: Lexington Books/D.C. Heath and Company, 1982). For a list of works about Mises, see page 5 of this.

For an introduction to the 'Austrian School' of economists, see Thomas C. Taylor, *The Fundamentals of Austrian Economics* (London: Adam Smith Institute, 1982).

6. The English edition is *Socialism* (London: Jonathan Cape, 1936).

7. For a sketch of the effects of inflation in Germany during this period, and for additional source material, see Robert Schuettinger and Eamonn Butler, *Forty Centuries of Wage and Price Controls* (Washington, D.C.: Heritage Foundation, 1979), pages 67-9.

8. John Maynard Keynes, *The General Theory of Employment, Interest and Money* (London: Macmillan, 1936).

9. Hayek's original outline of the idea, and his opening address to the first meeting at Mont Pelerin, are fortunately preserved as 'Historians and the Future of Europe' and 'Opening Address to a Conference at Mont Pelerin' in *Studies in Philosophy, Politics and Economics*, pages 135-59.

10. The Foreword to the 1956 paperback edition, in which Hayek makes

this point, is reproduced as '*The Road to Serfdom* after Twelve Years' in *Studies in Philosophy, Politics and Economics*, pages 216-28.

11. For a memoir of Hayek's activities at Chicago, see Fritz Machlup (ed.), *Essays on Hayek* (New York, New York University Press, 1976), pages 147-9.

12. Hayek took the opportunity of the Nobel Lecture to point out the limits to the knowledge of economists! The lecture is reprinted as 'The Pretence of Knowledge' in *New Studies*, pages 23-34.

13. A list of Hayek's principal works in English and other works referred to in the text can be found in the *Select bibliography* at the end of this book.

14. Arthur Shenfield, 'Friedrich A. von Hayek: Nobel Prizewinner', in Fritz Machlup (ed.), *Essays on Hayek* (New York: New York University Press, 1976), pages 171-6.

15. Schumpeter's remark is recalled by Hayek in 'The New Confusion about "Planning"' in *New Studies*, pages 235. Observing that he still comes across the same empty phrases more than thirty years after *The Road to Serfdom*, Hayek apologises 'in case . . . I should not be able to command quite the same patience and forbearance'.

16. Specifically, Hayek refers to ' . . . those little yet so important qualities which facilitate the intercourse between men in a free society: kindliness and a sense of humor, personal modesty, and respect for the privacy and belief in the good intentions of one's neighbor' (*The Road to Serfdom*, page 148; all page numbers quoted here refer to London editions).

Chapter 1: Understanding how society works

1. *The Constitution of Liberty*, Chapter 2, page 23.

2. This is the view which Hayek calls *constructivism*. One of Hayek's most significant contributions to the history of ideas has been to trace the history of this conception and show why it has such a hold over the minds of men. See particularly Chapter 1 of *Rules and Order*.

3. See 'The Errors of Constructivism' in *New Studies*, page 4; *Rules and Order*, page 20; and 'The Results of Human Action but not of Human Design' in *Studies in Philosophy, Politics and Economics*, page 96.

4. Hayek's powerful tracing back of this idea to the eighteenth-century Scottish philosophers and beyond can be found in 'The Results of Human Action but not of Human Design' in *Studies in Philosophy, Politics and Economics*, pages 96-105.

5. *Rules and Order*, pages 17-18; see also *The Constitution of Liberty*, pages 23-5: ' . . . man's mind is itself a product of the civilisation in which he has grown up and . . . it is unaware of much of the experience which has shaped it – experience that assists it by being embodied in the habits, conventions, language and moral beliefs which are part of its makeup'; and *New Studies*, pages 3-4: 'Man did not possess reason before civilisation. The two evolved together.'

6. For examples, see 'Notes on the Evolution of Systems of Rules of Conduct' in *Studies in Philosophy, Politics and Economics*, especially pages 69-70.

7. This example can be found in 'Scientism and the Study of Society', Chapter 4, in *The Counter-Revolution of Science*.

8. *The Constitution of Liberty*, Chapter 4, pages 69-70.

9. *New Studies*, pages 7-8, *Rules and Order*, Chapter 2.

10. The classical writers such as John Locke who developed the theory of liberalism certainly knew this (see *The Constitution of Liberty*, page 60), although many critics of liberty even today get confused on the point and assume that the unplanned liberal order must rely on people's interests being identical; an unlikely event. For Hayek's criticism of this mistake, see Chapter 2 below, especially the section on 'Reciprocal, not common purposes'.

11. *The Constitution of Liberty*, pages 25-9; 'Rules, Perception and Intelligibility' in *Studies in Philosophy, Politics and Economics*, especially pages 43-4; and *New Studies*, pages 9-10. On the subject of the special kind of knowledge contained in rules and the impossibility of explaining it because it is 'knowledge how' to act and not 'knowledge of' particular facts which can be communicated to other people, Michael Oakeshott (one of the leading modern philosophers of conservatism) cites an interesting Chinese parable of the wheelwright who continues to make wheels into his old age because he says his skill 'comes from the heart. It is a thing that cannot be put into words [rules]; there is an art in it that I cannot explain to my son. . . It must have been the same with the men of old. All that was worth handing on, died with them; the rest, they put in their books' (Michael Oakeshott, *Rationalism in Politics*; London: Methuen, 1962, pages 9-10). For an elaboration of the distinction between 'knowing how' and knowledge of facts, see Gilbert Ryle, 'Knowing How and Knowing That', *Proceedings of the Aristotelian Society*, 1945-6, and his *The Concept of Mind* (London: Penguin, 1949).

12. Hayek has explained his view that even our perception of the world is rule-guided in his main contribution to psychology, *The Sensory Order*, and in other essays. Nobody doubts that the human mind absorbs the information it gets through sensations, perceptions and images, and that these are filed away and classified in its various compartments. But Hayek argues that this organising function of the mind must be *prior* to perception of particular things, since all the information we get about the world has gone through this sorting process. And the sorting function itself will develop as the mind recognises new links or distinctions between past experiences.

This has two important implications for Hayek's theory of society. First, the mind sees the world in terms of rules and abstract relations between different things, so it is not surprising that we are able to recognise patterns without always being able to describe the particular things which make them up. 'Fair play' or 'rules of justice' may be like this. Second, we can only know the world as it is filtered through past experience, so we can only judge social institutions in terms of the web of past values and customs that has built up over human evolution. Any claim to be able to 'rationally' reconstruct society from scratch is therefore overstated. The point is dealt with later in this chapter. For Hayek's views on rule-guided perception, see 'The Primacy of the Abstract' in *New Studies*, pages 35-49; and his 'Rules, Perception and Intelligibility' in *Studies in Philosophy, Politics and Economics*, pages 43-65.

Hayek's view also enables us to understand why different people might disagree about what actions might be appropriate under a certain general rule, for example the rules of fair play. This is because the way in which our minds classify information 'is "subjective" in the sense of belonging to the perceiving subject', although our minds work rather similarly and we therefore find a reasonable measure of agreement in most such cases (*The Sensory Order*, page 23). For a brief exposition of Hayek's mental theories, see *The Sensory Order*, Chapter 2.

13. On the articulation of rules, see *Rules and Order*, pages 76-7; on the development of the common law, see *Rules and Order*, pages 81-8; Chapters 11-13 of *The Constitution of Liberty* treat the same subject much more broadly. 'The Confusion of Language in Political Thought', reproduced in *New Studies* (pages 71-97), has a short section on the articulation of rules on pages 81-2, and is useful because of other distinctions it makes which help to understand Hayek's separation of 'grown' and 'planned' societies.

14. Hayek, by contrast, considers these only 'the thin layer of rules, deliberately adopted or modified to serve known purposes' (*The Political Order of a Free People*, page 160).

15. According to the British philosopher and mathematician Alfred North Whitehead, 'Civilization advances by extending the number of important operations which we can perform without thinking about them' (quoted by Hayek at the head of Chapter 2 of *The Constitution of Liberty*; in *Individualism and Economic Order*, page 88; and in *The Counter-Revolution of Science*, page 154).

16. *Rules and Order*, pages 49-52.

17. For a demonstration of this, see *The Sensory Order*, pages 184-90.

18. '. . . we can never at one and the same time question all . . . values. Such absolute doubt could lead only to the destruction of our civilisation and – in view of the numbers to which economic progress has allowed the human race to grow – to extreme misery and starvation' (*New Studies*, page 19).

19. For Hayek's definition and defence of freedom, see especially *The Constitution of Liberty*, Chapter 1.

20. Some of the advantages of liberalism, with a general discussion of the subject, are set out in a neat form in 'Liberalism' in *New Studies*, pages 119-51, especially pages 132-51; 'The Principles of a Liberal Social Order' in *Studies in Philosophy, Politics and Economics*, pages 160-77, outlines a number of Hayek's main observations on the subject in a more compressed form.

21. *The Constitution of Liberty*, Chapter 2, especially page 38: 'The use of reason aims at control and predictability. But the process of the advance of reason rests on freedom and the unpredictability of human action.'

22. *Studies in Philosophy, Politics and Economics*, page 247.

23. And, of course, knowledge spreads quickly, to the benefit of all, because it is free: '. . . the free gift of the knowledge that has cost those in the lead much to achieve enables those who follow to reach the same level at a much smaller cost,' says Hayek in *The Constitution of Liberty*, page 47, arguing that the gift of

knowledge is one of the greatest benefits which rich countries can give to others. In a free society, Hayek would reform most of the restraints upon the sharing of knowledge: 'I am thinking here of the extension of the concept of property to such rights and privileges as patents for inventions, copyright, trade-marks and the like', which have done 'a great deal to foster the growth of monopoly', so that 'drastic reforms may be required if competition is to be made to work' (*Individualism and Economic Order*, pages 113-14). See also *The Constitution of Liberty*, page 265, and *The Road to Serfdom*, page 28. Sadly, Hayek does not elaborate much on this point.

24. See Chapter 3. 'It is no exaggeration to say that if we had to rely on conscious central planning for the growth of our industrial system, it would never have reached the degree of differentiation, complexity, and flexibility it has attained' (*The Road to Serfdom*, page 37).

25. *The Constitution of Liberty*, page 31.

26. *The Constitution of Liberty*, pages 20-21.

27. Note the crucial distinction between Hayek's liberalism and the *laissez-faire* caricature. The *laissez-faire* doctrine suggests that the less government intervention there is in society, and the smaller the body of law, the better it is. Hayek, however, argues that institutional arrangements are needed if freedom is to be protected: there is no 'natural harmony' which reconciles human interests without some body of institutions; see *The Constitution of Liberty*, page 60.

28. For a brief summary of the distinction between 'private' law (covering personal relationships and criminal law) and 'public' law (administrative and constitutional law), see *New Studies*, pages 76-80. The view, known as 'legal positivism', that there is no qualitative difference between the two kinds of law is today widespread; Hayek has criticised it on several occasions. According to this view, *all* law is a deliberate construction, serving particular purposes. For the positivist view, see Hans Kelsen, *What is Justice?* (Berkeley, California: 1957). Hayek's best attacks on this view are probably to be found in *The Constitution of Liberty*, pages 236-9, and (slightly more technical) *The Mirage of Social Justice*, pages 44-56.

29. *Rules and Order*, pages 77-8.

30. *Rules and Order*, page 81: the power of any early ruler 'rested largely on the expectation that he would enforce a law presumed to be given independently of him'.

31. *New Studies*, pages 10-11.

32. In *The Constitution of Liberty*, pages 139-40, Hayek calls this the 'private sphere', but in *Rules and Order*, pages 106-110, the concept is developed (more eloquently but more abstractly) as that of the 'protected domain'.

33. 'These general, abstract rules, which are laws in the substantive sense, are, as we have seen, essentially long-term measures, referring to yet unknown cases and containing no references to particular persons, places or objects. Such laws must always be prospective, never retrospective, in their effect' (*The Constitution of Liberty*, page 208). An account of the characteristics of the rule of law comprises Chapter 14 of that work.

34. *The Constitution of Liberty*, pages 218-19.

35. *New Studies*, pages 18-20. For change and development of 'private' law, see also *Rules and Order*, Chapter 5.

36. 'The Three Sources of Human Values', reproduced as an Epilogue in *The Political Order of a Free People*, pages 153-76.

37. *New Studies*, page 11.

38. Hayek uses the phrase, first used by Adam Smith, in the same sense as the term 'Open Society' coined by Sir Karl Popper in *The Open Society and its Enemies* (London: Routledge, 1945).

39. *The Mirage of Social Justice*, pages 133-4.

40. *The Mirage of Social Justice*, page 90.

Chapter 2: The market process

1. 'The Pretence of Knowledge', *New Studies*, page 34.

2. Hayek's main development of this idea can be found in Chapter 10 of *The Mirage of Social Justice*. Other contributions on the use of knowledge in the economy can be found in 'The Use of Knowledge in Society' in *Individualism and Economic Order*, pages 77-91; and on competition, 'The Meaning of Competition' in *Individualism and Economic Order*, pages 92-106, and 'Competition as a Discovery Procedure' in *New Studies*, pages 179-90.

The idea that we derive economic benefits by co-operating with people who are motivated not by our advantage but by their own, is crucial to an understanding of the market exchange process. It goes back to the famous remark of Adam Smith that 'It is not from the benevolence of the butcher, the brewer or the baker that we expect our dinner, but from their regard to their own interests' (*The Wealth of Nations*, London: Dent Everyman edition, 1975 page 13).

3. Hayek calls this a *catallaxy*, a system of exchange (based on the Greek word for exchange); see 'The Confusion of Language in Political Thought' in *New Studies*, especially pages 90-92, and *The Mirage of Social Justice*, Chapter 10.

4. *The Mirage of Social Justice*, pages 112-13.

5. 'This particular function of government is somewhat like that of a maintenance squad in a factory, its object being not to produce any particular services or products to be consumed by the citizens, but rather to see that the mechanism which regulates the production of those goods and services is kept in good working order' (*Rules and Order*, page 47).

6. *The Mirage of Social Justice*, pages 115-16.

7. *Individualism and Economic Order*, pages 85-6.

8. *Individualism and Economic Order*, pages 86-7.

9. For these examples, see *Individualism and Economic Order*, page 80. Even the 'much maligned speculators' (*The Mirage of Social Justice*, page 116) play a valuable role in spreading this kind of fleeting information through the economic system.

10. In *1980s Unemployment and the Unions*, page 34, Hayek stresses the social benefits produced by aiming at the least costly production methods:

'Producing cheaply means using as few resources as possible, measured in terms of the rates (prices) at which different products could be substituted for each other in their various uses. And reducing costs means setting free resources which could produce more elsewhere. In any particular instance, the primary aim must therefore always be to use as few resources as possible for a given output. Only as a result of producing as cheaply as possible will people have income to spare to pay for the work of others.' Yet much of the employment policy of Western governments, he suggests, has been directed at the use of as much labour as possible, which must be a loss to humanity – 'socially loss-making', as Hayek puts it.

11. For Hayek's analysis of the cattalactics of substitution, see *The Mirage of Social Justice*, pages 117-20.

12. *Individualism and Economic Order*, page 87.

13. *1980s Unemployment and the Unions*, page 42. On the point that the market rewards what *ought to be done* and not what labour is already invested, see also *The Mirage of Social Justice*, pages 116-17.

14. *The Mirage of Social Justice*, pages 119-20.

15. *Individualism and Economic Order*, page 88.

16. Hayek would not claim exclusive credit for his critique of static equilibrium theory and the theory of entrepreneurship and competition. Much of it is due to the efforts of many members of the 'Austrian School', of which Hayek forms a part. See especially Israel M. Kirzner, *Competition and Entrepreneurship* (Chicago: Chicago University Press, 1973). For Hayek's treatment, see especially *New Studies*, pages 179-90, and *Individualism and Economic Order*, pages 77-106.

17. *Individualism and Economic Order*, page 95.

18. *Individualism and Economic Order*, page 99.

19. That is, where the marginal rates of substitution between any two factors of production become equal in all their uses; see *The Mirage of Social Justice*, page 118.

20. The problem was initially tackled in *Prices and Production*, and again (with slightly different assumptions) in *Monetary Theory and the Trade Cycle*. For later work on the problem, see 'The Campaign against Keynesian Inflation' in *New Studies*, pages 191-231. Of a less strictly academic nature is *1980s Unemployment and the Unions*, which covers several aspects of employment and monetary policy.

21. Hayek has long resisted the customary preoccupation with averages and aggregates in economic thinking. An aggregate such as the general level of prices, the quantity of money or the rate of unemployment attempts to lump together things which cannot be summed up in statistics. Moreover, it is only particular circumstances which affect people's behaviour, not these aggregates: 'For none of these magnitudes *as such* ever exerts an influence on the decisions of individuals . . .' (*Prices and Production*, pages 4-5).

22. *Prices and Production*, page 3.

23. *New Studies*, page 173.

24. *Profits, Interest and Investment*, page 24. For Hayek's views on Keynesian

policies, see especially *New Studies*, pages 191-231.

25. *1980s Unemployment and the Unions*, page 16.

26. *1980s Unemployment and the Unions*, page 57.

27. For a penetrating summary of this view, see *A Tiger by the Tail*, pages 113-19.

28. *1980s Unemployment and the Unions*, page 23.

29. *The Constitution of Liberty*, pages 338-9.

Chapter 3: Hayek's critique of socialism

1. *The Road to Serfdom*, page 23.

2. *The Road to Serfdom*, page 3.

3. See '*The Road to Serfdom* after Twelve Years' in *Studies in Philosophy, Politics and Economics*, pages 216-28, for Hayek's view on this.

4. Quoted by Hayek at the head of Chapter 9 of *The Road to Serfdom*.

5. Hayek's *Road to Serfdom* inspired a number of popular discussions of this phenomenon, the most graphic of which is probably George Orwell's *1984*. Orwell had earlier reviewed Hayek's book in *The Observer*.

6. *The Road to Serfdom*, page 4.

7. Edmund Burke, *Reflections on the Revolution in France* (1790).

8. *The Road to Serfdom*, page 102.

9. This is a good place to begin for anyone who is on the front line of political argument.

10. *The Road to Serfdom*, pages 33-4.

11. It is noteworthy that Marx was never good at predicting the development and fall of capitalism: he argued that socialist revolutions would occur in the most advanced industrial economies, when in fact they have occurred predominantly in rural ones. But, as Hayek has observed, it is more likely that collectivist controls will work in an agricultural economy, where there are fewer products and therefore less information to be manipulated by the planning authorities.

12. For a discussion of monopoly, see *The Political Order of a Free People*, especially pages 72-88.

13. *Individualism and Economic Order*, page 91.

14. *Individualism and Economic Order*, page 83.

15. 'It is because it was not dependent on organization but grew up as a spontaneous order that the structure of modern society has attained that degree of complexity which it possesses and which far exceeds any that could have been achieved by deliberate organization' (*Rules and Order*, page 51).

16. For Hayek's development and critique of this moderate planning proposal, see 'The New Confusion about "Planning"' in *New Studies*, pages 232-46, especially pages 238-40.

17. *New Studies*, page 23.

18. *New Studies*, page 240.

19 *Individualism and Economic Order*, page 79.

20. *The Road to Serfdom*, pages 40-41.

21. *The Road to Serfdom*, page 46.

22. *The Constitution of Liberty*, page 116.

23. All of these things have been seen in, for example, land development planning agencies in Britain. For criticism of this, see *The Constitution of Liberty*, Chapter 22: Hayek suggests that 'The administrative despotism to which town planners are inclined to subject the whole economy is well illustrated by the drastic provisions of the British Town and Country Planning Acts of 1947' (*The Constitution of Liberty*, page 353).

24. *The Constitution of Liberty*, page 262.

25. *The Road to Serfdom*, page 65.

26. *The Road to Serfdom*, pages 68-9.

27. *The Constitution of Liberty*, pages 297-300, is instructive on this point. See also Chapter 5 below.

28. *The Road to Serfdom*, page 10.

29. *The Road to Serfdom*, page 80.

30. For examples of how income redistribution has favoured organised voting groups and not the genuinely poor, see *The Constitution of Liberty*, pages 311-13, especially page 313: '. . . once the principle of proportional taxation is abandoned, it is not necessarily those in greatest need but more likely the classes with the greatest voting strength that will profit. . .'

31. For Hayek's analysis of this point, see *The Road to Serfdom*, Chapter 10.

32. *The Road to Serfdom*, Chapter 11.

33. Quoted on the cover of the 1956 American edition of *The Road to Serfdom* and on the 1976 British reprint.

34. See '*The Road to Serfdom* after Twelve Years' in *Studies in Philosophy, Politics and Economics*, pages 216-28.

Chapter 4: The criticism of social justice

1. *New Studies*, page 57. The main sources for Hayek's critique of the social justice idea are: *The Mirage of Social Justice*, especially Chapters 8 and 9; *The Constitution of Liberty*, Chapter 6; 'The Atavism of Social Justice' in *New Studies*, pages 57-68; and 'What is "Social"? What does it Mean?' in *Studies in Philosophy, Politics and Economics*, pages 237-47.

2. *Studies in Philosophy, Politics and Economics*, page 221.

3. This is usually known as 'commutative' justice. See *The Mirage of Social Justice*, pages 31-3.

4. One is reminded of the example of Bertrand de Jouvenel: 'Taken to see a steel furnace, a small child or a savage may be terrified by its roaring and call it "wicked". This view, however, will be dropped as soon as it is understood that the furnace has no spirit. No informed person will think of the furnace as evil because it is fiercely red, lets out occasional streams of burning lava, and feeds on gritty scrap iron and coal that is black. It is merely a device, instrumentally good, since it leads to the production of tools and machines, serving men's purposes' (*Capitalism and the Historians*, page 93).

5. *The Mirage of Social Justice*, page 69.

6. *Studies in Philosophy, Politics and Economics*, pages 242-3. Hayek says earlier (page 238): 'the word "social" has become an adjective which robs of its clear meaning every phrase it qualifies and transforms it into a phrase of unlimited elasticity, the implications of which can always be distorted if they are unacceptable . . .'

7. *The Mirage of Social Justice*, page 67.

8. *The Political Order of a Free People*, page 151.

9. *The Mirage of Social Justice*, pages 77-8.

10. A point made in *The Road to Serfdom*, page 76. It should be noted that although justice is supposed to be 'blind', this is a point in its favour. The market process is also 'blind', and provides far more opportunities for minority groups and others who might be discriminated against in a less impartial system. On this point, see also Milton Friedman, *Capitalism and Freedom* (Chicago: University of Chicago Press, 1962), Chapter 7.

11. *The Constitution of Liberty*, page 94.

12. Hayek puts this bluntly in *The Constitution of Liberty*, pages 96-7.

13. *The Mirage of Social Justice*, page 78.

14. *The Political Order of a Free People*, page 150. The strength of Hayek's criticism of a political system which is so dependent on placating sectional interests comes out strongly in this volume, and is revealing.

15. *The Political Order of a Free People*, page 103.

16. On this point, see *Studies in Philosophy, Politics and Economics*, page 245.

17. *The Mirage of Social Justice*, pages 88-91. On the nationalism of collectivists, see *The Road to Serfdom*, pages 104-7.

18. *The Constitution of Liberty*, pages 44-6, contains Hayek's main arguments on this intelligent point.

19. For these, see *The Constitution of Liberty*, pages 124-30.

20. *The Mirage of Social Justice*, page 85.

21. *The Constitution of Liberty*, pages 90-91.

22. Possibly Hayek has in mind here the building up of a family business in two or three generations, which would have been impossible in only one, or the gradual acceptance of a new culture or set of social values, which is often resisted by the first generation but absorbed by succeeding ones.

23. *The Mirage of Social Justice*, page 137.

24. Hayek does not stress the motive of envy, although he quotes John Stuart Mill on it being 'the most anti-social and evil of all the passions' (*The Constitution of Liberty*, page 93; and again in *The Mirage of Social Justice*, page 98, and *Studies in Philosophy, Politics and Economics*, page 245). It is partly because of this foundation of envy, but principally because of the gross misunderstanding of the idea of social justice, that Hayek is able to say that 'a great deal of what today professes to be social is, in the deeper and truer sense of the word, thoroughly and completely anti-social' (*Studies in Philosophy, Politics and Economics*, page 247).

25. *The Political Order of a Free People*, page 165. On a similar point, see *1980s Unemployment and the Unions*, page 43.

26. *The Reactionary Character of the Socialist Conception* (Stanford, California:

Hoover Institution, 1978), page 3.

27. *New Studies*, page 67.

28. *The Mirage of Social Justice*, page 97.

Chapter 5: The institutions of a liberal order

1. *The Road to Serfdom*, page 14.

2. *Rules and Order*, page 32.

3. One passage in particular summarises Hayek's position on the proper role of a liberal government: 'The central concept of liberalism is that under the enforcement of universal rules of just conduct, protecting a recognizable private domain of individuals, a spontaneous order of human activities of much greater complexity will form itself than could ever be produced by deliberate arrangement, and that in consequence the coercive activities of government should be limited to the enforcement of such rules, whatever other services government may at the same time render by administering those particular resources which have been placed at its disposal for those purposes' (*Studies in Philosophy, Politics and Economics*, page 162).

4. *The Political Order of a Free People*, page 139.

5. *The Political Order of a Free People*, page 47. The development of cable television is obviously an instance of such a technical improvement. Road financing by meters in cars may be another example, an innovative way of making motorists bear costs in direct relationship to the costs and congestion they impose on the road system. Private provision of many services financed by national and local government reminds us that there is also no reason for most services to be retained as a government monopoly.

6. *The Constitution of Liberty*, Chapter 20, especially page 306: 'In many ways I wish I could omit this chapter. Its argument is directed against beliefs so widely held that it is bound to offend many.'

7. For Hayek's criticism, see especially *The Constitution of Liberty*, Chapter 18, and *1980s Unemployment and the Unions*.

8. *The Constitution of Liberty*, page 275.

9. For this point, see *1980s Unemployment and the Unions*, pages 53-4.

10. *1980s Unemployment and the Unions*, page 51.

11. *The Mirage of Social Justice*, pages 84-5.

12. Of course, many of the monopoly powers existing in Western countries are sanctioned by government or are given to government services, making them even more difficult to deal with. We must remember that 'All monopolists are notoriously uneconomical, and the bureaucratic machinery of government even more so. . .' (*The Constitution of Liberty*, page 346).

13. For details of this proposal, see Hayek's *Denationalisation of Money*.

14. Currency issuance has by no means always been a government monopoly. A system of private issuance and bill discounting operated very successfully in parts of the United States between 1825 and 1858, for example; see George Trivoli, *The Suffolk Bank* (London: The Adam Smith Institute, 1979).

15. *The Political Order of a Free People*, pages 57-8.

16. For this, see *Individualism and Economic Order*, pages 113-14.

17. See *The Constitution of Liberty*, pages 225-6.

18. The *Constitution of Liberty*, page 227. Hayek treats the same subject in *The Political Order of a Free People*, page 62, where he seems to suggest a larger role for government agencies.

19. *The Political Order of a Free People*, pages 54-6. Hayek also suggests that the open society may need this new form of risk minimisation to replace the sharing ethos of the tribal group, and to induce people to accept the advantages of the modern system.

20. This is suggested in *The Constitution of Liberty*, page 286. But there is more criticism of existing practices in Hayek's remarks than there is unequivocal statement of alternative proposals.

21. On health, see *The Constitution of Liberty*, pages 297-300.

22. *The Constitution of Liberty*, Chapter 24; *The Political Order of a Free People*, pages 60-62.

23. See *The Constitution of Liberty*, Chapter 22. A fascinating case study of the effects of rent control in Hayek's native Austria in his 'Austria: The Repercussions of Rent Restrictions', in *Verdict on Rent Control* (London: Institute of Economic Affairs, 1972), pages 1-17.

24. Another example is building regulations. Although these may sometimes be justified in terms of public safety, Hayek feels that they tend to be phrased for use with current levels of technology and often make future improvements impossible: 'Wherever such regulations go beyond the requirement of minimum standards, and particularly where they tend to make what at the given time and place is the standard method the only permitted method, they can become serious obstructions to desirable economic developments' (*The Constitution of Liberty*, page 355).

Chapter 6: The constitution of a liberal state

1. *The Political Order of a Free People*, page 128.

2. *New Studies*, pages 98-9. This essay, 'The Constitution of a Liberal State', is an intriguing early outline (1967) of the ideas which were later developed in the third volume of *Law, Legislation and Liberty*.

3. For example *nomos* and *thesis*, *private law* and *public law*, and, perhaps confusingly, *law* and *legislation*. See 'The Confusion of Language in Political Thought' in *New Studies*, pages 71-97, especially Section 2; *Rules and Order*, Chapters 5 and 6.

4. For Hayek's separation of *will* and *opinion* and its importance in social theory, see *New Studies*, pages 82-8. The confusion is a crucial shortcoming in the works of Rousseau, who in consequence argues for 'sovereign' (i.e. tyrannical) powers for an assembly of the people.

5. 'Formal rules are thus merely instrumental in the sense that they are expected to be useful to yet unknown people, for purposes for which these people will decide to use them, and in circumstances which cannot be

foreseen in detail' (*The Road to Serfdom*, page 56).

6. See *The Constitution of Liberty*, Chapter 11, and *Rules and Order*, pages 82-5.

7. As an illustration, Hayek says that the law in the sense of a rule of just conduct cannot be 'carried out' or 'executed' as an administrative measure can be. True laws are not directions to do particular things, but rules of acting in a general way (*Rules and Order*, pages 126-8).

8. *The Political Order of a Free People*, page 104.

9. *The Political Order of a Free People*, page 31.

10. 'It is also possible for reasonable people to argue that the ideals of democracy would be better served if, say, all the servants of government or all recipients of public charity were excluded from the vote.' (*The Constitution of Liberty*, page 105).

11. The most detailed treatment of democracy by Hayek can be found in Chapter 7 of *The Constitution of Liberty*. Further remarks on the same subject occur in *The Political Order of a Free People*, pages 133-46; and, briefly, in *New Studies*, pages 92-7.

12. *The Road to Serfdom*, page 52.

13. *The Political Order of a Free People*, page 103.

14. *The Constitution of Liberty*, page 112.

15. *The Political Order of a Free People*, page 134.

16. *The Political Order of a Free People*, page 102.

17. *The Constitution of Liberty*, page 403.

18. For Hayek's views on the rule of law, see especially *The Constitution of Liberty*, Chapter 14, and *The Road to Serfdom*, Chapter 6.

19. This is a development of Hayek's earlier view that 'The rule of law requires that the executive in its coercive action be bound by rules which prescribe not only when and where it may use coercion but also in what manner it may do so. The only way in which this can be ensured is to make all its actions of this kind subject to judicial review' (*The Constitution of Liberty*, page 211).

20. It was age 40 in the 1967 paper, 'The Constitution of a Liberal State' (*New Studies*, page 103), but this figure is from *The Political Order of a Free People*, page 113. Hayek's explanation of his model constitution occurs in Chapter 17 of that work.

21. *New Studies*, page 103.

Epilogue: Sense and sorcery in the social sciences

1. *The Counter-Revolution of Science*, page 77.

2. 'Scientism and the Study of Society' first appeared in *Economica* between 1941 and 1944, together with a related work, 'The Counter-Revolution of Science', which traced the errors of several prominent social theorists. These essays are now collected in *The Counter-Revolution of Science*. Other criticisms of the misuse of scientific method can be found in 'The Pretence of Knowledge' (with special reference to economics) in *New Studies*, pages 23-34, and in various parts of *Individualism and Economic Order*, especially Chapter 3.

3. *New Studies*, page 30.

4. For these examples, see *The Counter-Revolution of Science*, Chapter 2.

5. Social sciences can be described, therefore, as having an inherently 'subjective' nature (*The Counter-Revolution of Science*, Chapter 3). Unfortunately this term has connotations that it is not respectable, connotations deliberately fostered by those who presume social science can be more 'objective' than it can.

6. In this regard, see especially Karl Popper, *The Poverty of Historicism* (London: Routledge, 1961). This is a difficult book, but its influence in ridding the social studies of historicism was probably greater than Hayek's, although the two undoubtedly reinforced each other.

7. These examples are not from Hayek but from Arthur Shenfield, 'Scientism and the Study of Society', in Fritz Machlup (ed.), *Essays on Hayek* (New York: New York University Press, 1976).

8. See *The Counter-Revolution of Science*, Chapter 7, for a fuller treatment of this rather complicated subject.

9. For a difficult but perceptive treatment of the study of complex structures, see 'The Theory of Complex Phenomena' in *Studies in Philosophy, Politics and Economics*, pages 22-42.

10. See 'The Intellectuals and Socialism' in *Studies in Philosophy, Politics and Economics*, pages 178-94.

11. *The Road to Serfdom*, page xi.

12. *Studies in Philosophy, Politics and Economics*, page 194.

Select Bibliography

Listed below (arranged chronologically by original date of publication) are Hayek's main works in English which are mentioned in the text. More information on in-print titles can be obtained from Laissez Faire Books, 532 Broadway, New York, N.Y. 10012. For a more complete list of Hayek's pamphlets and articles up to 1976, see Fritz Machlup (ed.), *Essays on Hayek* (New York: New York University Press, 1976), pages 51–59.

Prices and Production. 1931. Fairfield, N.J.: Augustus M. Kelley, 1967.

Monetary Theory and the Trade Cycle. 1933. Fairfield, N.J.: Augustus M. Kelley, 1975.

Profits, Interest and Investment, and Other Essays on the Theory of Industrial Fluctuation. 1939. Fairfield, N.J.: Augustus M. Kelley, 1975.

The Pure Theory of Capital. 1941. Chicago: University of Chicago Press, 1975.

The Road to Serfdom. 1944. Chicago: University of Chicago Press, 1956.

Individualism and Economic Order. Chicago: University of Chicago Press, 1948.

The Sensory Order: An Inquiry into the Foundations of Theoretical Psychology. Chicago: University of Chicago Press, 1952. Out of print. London: Routledge & Kegan Paul, 1976.

The Counter-Revolution of Science. 1952. Indianapolis: Liberty Press, 1979.

The Constitution of Liberty. Chicago: University of Chicago Press, 1960.

Studies in Philosophy, Politics and Economics. Chicago: University of Chicago Press, 1967.

Law, Legislation and Liberty.

☐ Vol. 1, *Rules and Order.* Chicago: University of Chicago Press, 1973.

☐ Vol. 2, *The Mirage of Social Justice.* Chicago: University of Chicago Press, 1976.

☐ Vol. 3, *The Political Order of a Free People.* Chicago: University of Chicago Press, 1979.

New Studies in Philosophy, Politics, Economics and the History of Ideas. Chicago: University of Chicago Press, 1978.

The Fatal Conceit. Chicago: University of Chicago Press, forthcoming.

OTHER WORKS (arranged alphabetically by title)

Capitalism and the Historians (ed.). Chicago: University of Chicago Press, 1954.

Choice in Currency: A Way to Stop Inflation. London: Institute of Economic Affairs, 1976. (Occasional Paper 48.)

Collectivist Economic Planning (ed.). Fairfield, N.J.: Augustus M. Kelley, 1976.

Confusion of Language in Political Thought. London: Institute of Economic Affairs. (Occasional Paper 20.)

The Denationalization of Money. London: Institute of Economic Affairs, 1978. (Hobart Paper 70.)

Economic Freedom and Representative Government. London: Institute of Economic Affairs. (Occasional Paper 39.)

Full Employment at Any Price. London: Institute of Economic Affairs, 1975. (Occasional Paper 45.)

Monetary Nationalism and International Stability. Fairfield, N.J.: Augustus M. Kelley, 1964.

1980s Unemployment and the Unions. London: Institute of Economic Affairs, 1980.

The Reactionary Character of the Socialist Conception. Stanford, Calif.: Hoover Institution Press, 1978.

A Tiger by the Tail: The Keynesian Legacy of Inflation. Washington: Cato Institute, 1979. (Cato Paper 6.)

Unemployment and Monetary Policy: Government as Generator of the "Business Cycle." Washington: Cato Institute, 1979.

INDEX

Austrian School, 3, 143-5, 151n, 157n

Banks, 8, 58-9, 115-16
Barry, Norman P., 151n
Behaviourism, 138
Burke, Edmund, 67, 158n
Business cycle, 3, 8-9
Butler, Eamonn, 151n

Capital, 58-60, 63, 69, 82, 101, 111, 112, 114, 120, 142
Capitalism, 38-9, 136, 139
Catallaxy (*see also* Market order), 156n, 157n
Chicago School, 6
Civilisation, 16, 18, 25, 34, 37, 102, 152n
Coercion, 10, 24, 27-8, 31, 55, 67, 76, 86, 95, 107-10, 112-14, 128-30, 163n
Collectivism, 82-4, 139-41, 158n
Competition, 26, 41, 51-5, 68-70, 111, 113-15, 145, 156n
Complexity, 9, 10, 16-9, 21-4, 25, 26, 30, 33, 51, 57, 71-2, 76, 88-90, 93, 106, 143, 144-8, 150, 155n, 159n, 161n, 164n
Conservatism, 19, 149-50
Constitution, 11, 121-5, 128-31

Defence, and security, 107-8, 117
Democracy, 66-8, 75-8, 119, 126-9, 163n

Education, 6, 119-20
Entrepreneurship, 54-5, 157n
Equality, 31, 32-3, 77-8, 80-81, 91, 94-5, 101-2, 123
Equilibrium, 55-7, 61, 157n
Evolution, 11, 16-17, 20-21, 24, 30, 33-40, 150, 152n

Freedom, *see* Liberty
Friedman, Milton, 119-20, 160n

Hayek, Friedrich A., influence of, 1, 11-12, 84-5
Hayek, Friedrich A., works cited
  Capitalism and the Historians, 5, 159n
  Collectivist Economic Planning, 9
  The Constitution of Liberty, 1, 6, 10-11, 121, 152n, 153n, 154n, 155n, 156n, 158n, 159n, 160n, 161n, 162n, 163n

The Counter-Revolution of Science, 4, 9, 153n, 154n, 163n, 164n
Denationalisation of Money, 161n
The Fatal Conceit, 7, 11, 36
Individualism and Economic Order, 9, 154n, 155n, 156n, 157n, 158n, 162n, 163n
Law, Legislation and Liberty, 1, 7, 10-11, 85, 107, 121, 162n; *see also* the titles of individual volumes
The Mirage of Social Justice, 155n, 156n, 157n, 159n, 160n, 161n
Monetary Theory and the Trade Cycle, 3, 8, 157n
1980s Unemployment and the Unions, 156n, 157n, 158n, 161n
New Studies in Philosophy, Politics, Economics and the History of Ideas, 152n, 153n, 154n, 155n, 156n, 157n, 158n, 159n, 161n, 162n, 163n, 164n
The Political Order of a Free People, 151n, 154n, 156n, 158n, 160n, 161n, 162n, 163n
Prices and Production, 3, 8, 157n
Profits, Interest and Investment, 8, 157n
The Pure Theory of Capital, 4, 8-9
The Reactionary Character of the Socialist Conception, 160-61n
The Road to Serfdom, 1, 4, 6, 9, 10, 12, 66, 68, 83, 84-5, 86, 121, 152n, 155n, 158n, 159n, 160n, 161n, 163n, 164n
Rules and Order, 152n, 153n, 154n, 155n, 156n, 158n, 163n
'Scientism and the Study of Society', 4, 132, 153n, 163n
The Sensory Order, 153n, 154n
Studies in Philosophy, Politics and Economics, 151n, 152n, 153n, 154n, 158n, 159n, 160n, 161n, 164n
A Tiger by the Tail, 158n
Health policy, 6, 79-80, 118-19, 162n
Historicism, 140-41
Housing, and rents, 120, 162n

Ideas, power of, 1, 11-12
Income and wealth, distribution of, 1, 80-81, 87, 91, 94-6, 97-107, 110
Inheritance, 101-2
Inflation, 3, 8, 58-61, 63-5, 115-16, 151n
Intellectuals, and socialism, 148-50, 164n

de Jouvenel, Bertrand, 159n
Justice (*see also* Social justice), 21, 28-33, 50, 76-8, 86-8, 100, 105, 122-6, 129, 160n

167